the incredible australian
ICE CREAM
book

Elise Pascoe

Decalon

FOREWORD

The Incredible Australian Ice Cream Book — What an ambitious title this is. But then the concept of it was ambitious from the start. The love of her task and the great enthusiasm which goes to make up the author — Elise Pascoe — has made this book quite incredible. I certainly hope when you have read it and continuously used it as a reference or handbook in your kitchen, then you too will believe it is aptly named.

In my travels throughout the world, I have found many places which are not necessarily great dairy-producing areas, but where the consumers in those places do have a greater choice of dairy produce than that which has so far been appearing in Australia. In view of this I made a promise to myself and to all Australians who enjoy dairy products that with the passage of time and effort, I would endeavour to change that situation. This book and the products with which it deals is just one step towards honouring that promise.

In North America, making ice cream at home is a family affair. Children love helping (and tasting). Father makes whilst Mother mixes. Ice cream making days are fun days — just as much join-in fun as a family barbecue.

Australians are great ice cream eaters. Now the dairy industry is taking the initiative in making it easier and less expensive for ice cream to be produced in the home. Introduction of a creamy-smooth blend of milk and cream, similar to the American product called half and half, which we are calling Smoothy, and the appearance on the market of modern electric and hand-operated ice cream churns at attractive prices, will open up new and wider fields of demand.

Des Cooper
Chairman,
Victorian Dairy Industry Authority.

Publisher	Decalon Pty. Ltd. 320 Toorak Rd., South Yarra. 3141.
Originator	Ron Stephens
Editor	Bob Moors
Art Director	Harry Simon
Graphics	Warren Carter
Photography	John Street
Photographer's Assistant	Bill Anderson

© Copyright Decalon 1979
ISBN O 908074 14 X

Front cover photograph:
Left: Smoothy Vanilla Ice Cream with Brandied Fruit Sauce (see recipes pages 24 & 72).
Right: Apple Pie Ice Cream (see recipe page 25).
Biscuit: Langues de Chat (see recipe page 82).

Back cover photograph:
Left: Rocky Road Ice Cream (see recipe page 28).
Right: Frozen Plum Yoghurt (see recipe page 94).

Printed in Australia by Wilke & Co. Pty. Ltd.,
37-49 Browns Road, Clayton, Victoria.

CONTENTS

Milk is that fundamental element which accompanies man from the beginning to the end of his existence, and it cannot be substituted by any other element that is equally complete characteristically.

INTRODUCTION

There are few sounds more enticing than the swish of an ice cream churn, cranking away in the background.

It conjures up wonderful ideas of silken, smooth, sensuous ice creams. Old favourites, new flavours and fantastic creations.

You may well ask, "Why make ice cream at home when you can buy a host of flavours and combinations?" Well, let me be the first to tell you that home made ice cream is a new taste thrill. It's incredible — quite easy to make, fun to do, and rewarding to serve. Whole families are making ice cream, and they're loving it. Work your way through the recipes in this book and discover that ice cream is no longer just a summer treat but a year-round favourite. And if you plan carefully it can be economical too.

THE HISTORY OF ICE CREAM

The first people to use ices, or ice creams, were the Chinese and they, in turn, taught the art to the Indians, Persians and Arabs.

Sicily, the island off the southern coast of Italy was invaded by the Arabs, who passed on to the Sicilians many of their habits, including ice cream making.

It was a Sicilian who took ice cream to France when, in 1660, Francesco Procopio brought the knowledge of sherbets to Paris. Sherbets are the most ancient of all ice creams. Called sorbetto in Italy, they are thought to have come from a drink the Arabs made called Sciarrot, which was pronounced sciorbet. It sounds rather like sherbet.

Information which dates back to the days of the Roman Empire, tells that Nero Claudius Caesar dined on a mixture of snow, honey and spices. He employed swift runners to bring snow from the mountains which was flavoured with fruit juices at his palace. These were the first water ices in Rome and were served half way through the meal to prepare the stomach for the numerous and heavy foods to follow.

In the thirteenth century Marco Polo discovered recipes for frozen milk desserts among the treasures he brought back from the court of the great Khan.

But it was in France a few centuries later, that ices had really become fashionable. Francesco Procope, now with a French accented name, had opened the first Parisienne ice cream parlour. Within a very short time, there were some two hundred and fifty such parlours. From France, ice cream making spread to the English court.

But in Paris, ice cream was changing. For the first time it was being made with a base of eggs and syrup. This led to the creation of more elaborate sweets, and by the end of the eighteenth century, the manufacture of "ice bombes" developed, and the savouring of ices became fashionable. The first ice cream parlours were opened in New York at this time.

In 1846, an American woman, Nancy Johnson, devised a freezer with a crank and a dasher. All this time, ice cream had been frozen by hand in a metal can contained in an ice-filled bucket. Her invention helped the beginning of commercial ice cream making.

In the mid nineteenth century, America's first wholesale ice cream factory was founded. Before long, there were several more, and from then on, the popularity of ice cream grew, unchecked. Technical advances included pasteurisation in 1895 and homogenisation in the early part of this century.

By this time the success of the Italian ice cream makers in Paris had grown steadily, and the quality of both creams and sherbets had improved markedly. By now, desserts based on ice cream had acquired great importance, replacing both traditional pastries and fresh cheeses.

For the first time the "Omelette Norvegienne" (Bombe Alaska) was served at a very important banquet. It is rumoured that it comes from the United States, but it made its official appearance at the Hotel de Paris in Montecarlo around 1895, prepared by a Mr Giroix. Its presentation was somewhat of a shock for the guests, due to its seemingly absurd principle, the combination of hot and cold elements.

At the turn of this century, coupes, mousses and parfaits began to appear as everyone became more creative and adventurous with ice cream. Until the first years of the twentieth century ice cream was made only for the most sumptuous banquets or elegant hotels where it gave the gatherings a touch of class. Of course during Nero's time, these preparations could only be made when snow was on the ground.

The development of ice cream on a mass-produced, commercial basis is partly as a result of the invention of the edible cone. In New Jersey in 1896, an Italian named Marchionni had the idea of wrapping a piece of pasta into a cone, in order to be able to fill it with ice cream and then eat it with the least possible difficulty! The Americans claim the invention for their own. It made its first public debut at the St. Louis World's Fair in 1904.

We've come a long way since the early days of iced desserts. So if you've never made ice cream before, you'll appreciate the easy operation of the modern ice cream churn, and the convenience of ices made at home with dairy products — to enrich your daily diet.

5

DAIRY PRODUCTS — A SOURCE OF FOOD

WHOLE MILK (full cream milk) is nearly a complete food for man. Milk, which is 13% solids, and 87% water, contains, in variable amounts, all the nutrients necessary for man's health and well being. Milk is a good source of high-quality protein; fat for energy; milk sugar (lactose) for energy and brain nutrition in infants; fat soluble vitamins; water soluble vitamins (especially riboflavin); and minerals (especially calcium, phosphorus and potassium).

SMOOTHY is a pasteurised, homogenised blend of full-cream milk and pure cream enriched with non-fat dry milk to a smooth creamy taste with pleasant body. The fat content is between that of full cream milk and light cream.

Making home made ice cream with Smoothy is like discovering hot water for the first time. The milk-cream blend of Smoothy lends itself to a smooth-textured ice cream with a delicious taste. It is available at milk bars, delicatessens and supermarkets.

Smoothy was developed and produced by the Victorian Dairy Industry Authority, and is similar to the Half and Half dairy products which have been popular in North America for many years.

Smoothy has a taste and texture just like its name and is ideal on breakfast cereals, in tea or coffee, as a topping on fresh or canned fruits and other desserts. As an ice cream ingredient, Smoothy has produced some exciting results as you'll find in the recipes ahead.

Take a tip and make the ice cream mixture a day ahead to give it time to gather flavour and to chill thoroughly before churning or setting. This way it will set far more quickly, resulting in smoother ice cream.

Homemade ice creams do not have the keeping qualities of commercially-prepared ices. Therefore they are best eaten the day they are made. The mixtures can be made up a day ahead and kept well-chilled until freezing time.

For good results when making ice cream, it is necessary to use top quality, fresh ingredients. Whereas for good storage, hygiene is the prime factor. The utensils and containers along with the preparation area must be of the cleanest standard possible.

"SKINNY" Skim Milk, from which most of the cream has been removed retains all of the natural goodness of whole milk, apart from the fat and fat-soluble vitamins. Because of the extremely low fat content, 0.1% or less, the energy content of "Skinny" is only half of that of full cream milk.

BIG M flavoured milks are blends of freshly pasteurised and homogenised whole milk and pasteurised flavour syrups.

Big M retains all the goodness of full cream milk, with the added bonus of specially formulated flavourings for that great taste sensation.

Big M Egg Flip is a pasteurised and homogenised blend of full cream milk, pure cream, pasteurised egg yolk, non-fat dry milk, flavouring (including sugar) and colouring. Egg Flip has all the goodness of full cream milk plus extra vitamins and minerals derived from the cream, egg yolk and non-fat dry milk.

WHICH ICE CREAM TO CHOOSE

There are numerous types of ice creams, from very rich to very lean. Choose an ice cream to suit your diet, your pocket and the time you have available. If making in advance, choose one which will keep. For convenience I have grouped them in the following sections.

SMOOTHY ICE CREAMS are very lean as they have no added cream and most require no cooking. They are reasonably smooth and delicious, and best eaten the day they are made. Maximum storage time is 5 days. Don't use Smoothy for making highly acidic ice creams unless you add extra enrichment, like cream or eggs. Smoothy produces a medium-smooth textured ice cream (see photo page 14). It is also the cheapest.

SMOOTHY ICE CREAMS WITH CREAM. Every one of the recipes in this section has additional cream. About half require some cooking. They store reasonably well, but are still best eaten the day they are made or the day after. Maximum storage is 2 weeks. Smoothy with cream makes a splendid base for most flavours. With additional cream, Smoothy produces a smooth ice cream (see photo page 26). It is a little more expensive.

CREAM ICE CREAMS. Are extremely rich with a cream base, very easy to work with, and very smooth. They require no churning and are best with flavourings which are not too rich. Probably the quickest to make of all the ice creams, so for the busy person, a wonderful asset. However, they can be expensive. Keep 3 weeks.

CUSTARD-BASED ICE CREAMS. Very rich, very smooth, they all need cooking and are best eaten one day after making. They keep for two weeks. Called Parfait Ice Cream in France and Mantecati in Italy, they are ideal bases for tortes, cakes, sundaes and coupes because they go so well with fruits (see photo page 36). These require no churning.

SKINNY SHERBETS, are ices made with a very low fat content. Just 0.1% butter fat, they are ideal for weight watchers, providing the flavourings are naturally low in kilojoules. A sugar substitute can be used for sweetening. These sherbets are extremely lean, therefore the texture is rather granular, as you would expect in a water ice. Sorbets or gelati, which are water ices, don't have space in this book as I have concentrated on the use of dairy products. Skinny sherbets, are deliciously refreshing and make a perfect ending to a rich meal. They are used in bombes (see photograph of Bombe Victoria page 52) and make an interesting change in sundaes, coupes and parfaits. Skinny Sherbets are the least expensive of all the ices in this book. They store well for 3 weeks but are best eaten the day they are made, require heating in some recipes but no actual cooking. Some need stabilising with gelatine and all are superior if churned.

ICE CREAM COMBINATIONS

PARFAITS are layered sundaes served in tall glasses. Parfaits can be made ahead and stored, frozen, for several hours before serving. One litre (4 cups) of ice cream will make approximately 7 parfaits. To clear any confusion, parfait also describes a custard-based ice cream. See my notes on "Which ice cream to choose."

SUNDAES AND COUPES are delicious combinations consisting of an ice cream base with fruits, cream and garnishes. Originally, coupes were served in silver or glass cups, which is why they are known as coupes in France and coppas in Italy. Champagne glasses, the saucer type, which have become unfashionable for serving champagne, make excellent serving dishes for coupes.

Sundaes may be presented in various ways with many different combinations and flavours. For small sundaes (single scoop) one litre (4 cups) of ice cream will serve 7 sundaes. For more elaborate sundaes, with several scoops of ice cream one litre will be enough for 3 or 4 sundaes.

The best known of all the classics must be Peach Melba. Created by August Escoffier in London, it is believed to be named after a famous Australian singer, Dame Nellie Melba. I have included it in the Grand Iced Desserts section of the recipes because it is a real favourite with guests.

All the recipes in this book have been devised so that expensive equipment is not necessary, but some equipment does make life easier and it is time saving.

The new electric ice cream maker gives us the chance to enjoy an enormous variety of mouth watering ice cream flavours made to individual family tastes. There are over 100 ice cream recipes to choose from, as well as frozen yoghurts. There are also recipes for accompaniments to ice creams, and I think you'll enjoy the recipes for yoghurts, and some others on dairy drinks.

CUSTARD-BASED ICE CREAMS

Custard-based ice creams are in fact, flavoured egg custards, which are then frozen. Therefore, it is important that we understand the basics of custard making.

It took me years to understand the intricacies of a good English custard; often called "boiled" custard, it should in fact never boil!

If you make custard regularly, until curdling becomes unthinkable, and follow these simple steps, before long you will be an expert. It's easy when you know how.

Make the custard with egg yolks and keep the whites for biscuits or for lightening ice creams. In the ice cream biscuit section there are several ideas for using left-over egg whites. A custard made with yolks, gives a smoother and richer result.

Before beginning decide on which type of saucepan to use. A heavy-based pan, preferably with sloping sides is best. These pans, which are designed for sauce making, are available at good cookware shops. The sloping sides allow the whisk to get into the "corners" of the pan. Use over a water bath (Bain marie) or asbestos mat or diffuser. A double saucepan is also acceptable. A word of warning on aluminium saucepans and using a wire whisk; beware of discolouration. Metal on metal can turn a light sauce or cream, grey.

Rinse the saucepan out with cold water before you begin. Don't dry it. This will prevent the fats in the milk sticking to the pan, and so ensure easier washing.

Choose either a whisk or a wooden spatula or spoon. Decide which suits you the best. I like to use a whisk, and I only made custards successfully when I changed from a spatula to a whisk.

THE FINER POINTS TO SUCCESSFUL CUSTARD MAKING:

1 Whisk or beat the yolks and sugar together until the mixture "ribbons". That is, when you lift the whisk or beaters above the mixture it leaves a ribbon trail. It must be pale and light.

2 Heat the milk, or Smoothy in the saucepan until it begins to rise in the pan. Immediately remove from the heat.

3 Pour a little of the hot milk onto the yolk mixture, whisking all the time. Pour into milk pan, place over medium heat and whisk gently, non stop, making sure the whisk covers the "corners". The custard must not

8

boil, or it will curdle. Cook until the custard thickens. If it shows signs of foaming and rising in the pan, immediately remove from the heat and beat furiously. Incorporating lots of air will reduce the temperature. After this, it can be left in the pan off the heat for a few minutes to continue to thicken in the heat of the pan.

4 To test if the custard is done, dip a wooden spoon into it, and run a finger through the custard on the spoon. If the line of separation doesn't join together again, the custard is thick enough and cooked.

5 If you do curdle the custard, don't despair. Though, a curdled custard is difficult to detect in ice cream, let's right it if we can. Immediately it is obvious the custard has curdled, drop one or two ice blocks into it, and whisk vigorously, to reduce the temperature of the over-heated custard and to dissolve the lumps (this method thins the custard a little). Or, vitamise it, then pass through a fine sieve.

6 To cool the custard without a skin forming on the top. Either whisk or stir over cold water until cool, or better still, because you are left free to attend to other tasks, is the paper method. Take a square of greaseproof paper and fold it diagonally, at least four times as though you were making a paper dart. Hold the "paper dart" horizontally over the top of the custard-making pan, and place the point over the centre. Measure the distance to the inner edge of the pan, and cut there. You now have a circle of paper cut to the correct size. Open it out and place directly on top of the custard so there is no air between the paper and custard. Leave to cool at room temperature or over cold water.

INGREDIENTS

EGGS

Eggs are used for enriching ice creams. Sometimes they are used raw which makes a delightful, light very easy ice cream. It's also very quick. Then there are ice creams which are custard based and with the exception of one recipe in this book, all the egg custard ice creams are made without flour.

Egg yolks are used alone in the custard base of the ice cream. The whites are sometimes whipped and added later in the recipe.

Some ice creams which are not custard based, have egg whites added to them. The correct way to incorporate the egg whites into the mixture, is to whip them so they form soft peaks. They should then be folded into the nearly set mixture. If you are using one of the three ice cream churns mentioned earlier, you should fold the egg whites into the mixture in the canister using a rubber spatula. This should be done 10 minutes before the ice cream finishes churning. Experience will tell you when this stage is reached. Obviously it would be difficult to fold egg whites into any icy mixture. It should be showing signs of setting but still fairly slushy.

Egg whites are used in this manner for aerating the ice cream. They lighten the texture of the ice cream, also the colour and of course the flavour. This must be remembered when you are preparing the ice cream mixture, knowing that egg whites will be added at a very late stage there must be plenty of flavour in the base mixture.

Many of the egg-based recipes use the yolks only. Therefore, I have included a few recipes for using the left-over egg whites. The section on ice-cream biscuits will give you some ideas.

CREAM

There are three different types of cream on the market. They are reduced cream (25% butter fat), thickened cream (35% butter fat), and pure cream (45% butter fat).

Use thickened cream because it whips well and gives a smoother result as it incorporates air into the cream and distributes the fats evenly. It is ideal for flavouring too.

Cream is also used for enriching ice creams as you will see in the second part of the ice cream chapter.

GELATINE

Gelatine powder is used as a stabiliser in several recipes. Mixtures which are extremely lean are often improved with a stabiliser.

Working with gelatine is easy as long as you always use it at blood temperature, that is when you feel neither hot nor cold to the touch by placing your finger in the ingredients. Or you can use a thermometer which should read 37°C (98.4°F).

Gelatine powder can be mixed in hot water, but it is essential that you dissolve the grains thoroughly. Then cool to blood temperature, add to ingredients which should be the same temperature or as near as possible. If you pour even hot gelatine into a large quantity of very cold mixture, you can be sure it will set in nasty little globules. Straining it out is the only solution. Then begin again and dissolve more gelatine.

FRUITS

After vanilla and chocolate, fruits must be the most popular ice cream flavourings. There are so many forms in which you can use fruits.

There are fresh fruits, stewed or poached fruits, preserved fruits, canned and pureed or frozen fruits. In this book I have devised a series of fruit ice creams using the best type of fruit processed in a manner which is suitable for the ice cream. I had many interesting experiences while creating ice creams in this area. For instance, fresh figs. I thought a fresh fig ice cream would be absolutely delicious. I was so wrong, it had a nasty after-taste. I discovered by using exactly the same ingredients and exactly the same quantities that if I gently stewed the fresh figs in the sugar first, I had a superb result. The difference of 10 minutes slow poaching of the fruit made all the difference.

There are fruits which will upset the freezing of ice cream. We all know that raw pineapple will not set in gelatine because of the high enzyme content. It, and a few other fruits upset freezing and must be cooked first. For a list of these fruits, see page 70 in the Problem Solving area. Naturally, each recipe deals with the fruit in question in the correct way before chilling and freezing the ice cream.

Cooking by the seasons is always wise. Therefore make the most of seasonal fruits. Some of the most delicious ice creams are made from berry fruits. By and large they have short seasons, so unless you use frozen or canned berries, you are not likely to be savouring these fruits in ice creams out of season.

Don't cook berries except green gooseberries (red ones can be used raw) and red and black currants, or you will lose that superb, fresh, tangy flavour.

To cook red and black currants and green gooseberries, poach in a light syrup of three parts water to one part sugar, for approximately 2 minutes for currants and 4 minutes for gooseberries, or until tender. Use very little syrup, just enough to cover the bottom of the pan. Don't discard the syrup, use it in the ice cream.

For successful fresh-fruit ice creams it is vital to use very ripe fruits with a pronounced perfume, otherwise, the flavours will not develop enough to come through the frozen ice cream. If you want to "put down" fresh fruits for out of season, you should be guided by one of the excellent books on freezing and preserving.

Jams and jellies made with fruits also make wonderful ice creams. They are amongst the quickest and most economical in this book as well as canned fruit ice cream. I have given you a basic recipe covering these ideas.

Some fruits are further enhanced by an essence or liqueur which helps to bring out the flavours. For instance, strawberries and Kirsch are sensational together.

LIQUEURS AND SPIRITS

Liqueurs and spirits compliment ice cream. Either frozen into the mixture or poured over the ice cream at the time of serving. In the summer it's important to chill the liqueur or spirit so that it doesn't melt the ice cream. Alcohol slows down the freezing process, because it sets at a lower temperature than the other ingredients. The best time to add alcohol to the ice cream mixture is approximately 10 minutes before churning is completed. In the freeze/beat method, add the alcohol at the time of beating half way through the setting process.

ESSENCES AND EXTRACTS

These should not be confused. Essences are synthetic flavourings. They are cheaper than pure extracts but much weaker, therefore they are false economy.

Some extracts are available from pharmacists, costing approximately twice that of synthetic flavourings, however you use two thirds less of the former in strength ratio. The best rule of how much to use is to work by taste. Extracts commonly available from pharmacists are peppermint, aniseed, lemon, orange and rose water.

Also available, is a very good range of imported extracts from West Germany. Use 1-4 drops compared to 1 teaspoon of the inexpensive essences. For best results, use extracts made from pure oils, not those labelled "imitation."

NUTS (KERNELS)

Make fantastic ice creams, but only almonds are commonly available already blanched.

The oily skins of some nuts tend to curdle the raw ice cream mixtures, particularly those with a very high fat content.

There are two ways to skin nuts. Either blanch in boiling water until the skins slip off, when pinched between finger and thumb. (This is the best method for most kernels, particularly for almonds and pistachios.)

Hazelnuts, however, are best roasted at 200°C (400°F) for 10-12 minutes or until the skins craze. Don't overcook them, they will catch as soon as the oils dry out. If you do burn them, they must be discarded for they will be bitter. Roasting them, intensifies the flavour and gives them a better texture.

Rub several together to test that the skins are loose, but beware they will be hot. When ready, leave to cool, then rub them together in your hands, loosening the skins.

CHOCOLATE

Is easy to use once you understand a few straight forward points.

Cooking chocolate is best for heating. You must not overheat it or the milk solids coagulate resulting in an impossible mess, which is irretrievable. So, it's wise to heat it gently over a shallow water bath which must never boil, and don't let it spit into the chocolate.

As soon as the chocolate melts, remove from the heat, but leave it in the water bath if you are not ready to use it. It can be kept warm this way for hours, providing you keep the water bath warm.

Chocolate garnishes are fun to make and not difficult, except in hot weather when they can be a bit tricky.

The chocolate dipping mixture is a triumph and very versatile. Use it for all kinds of ices and fruits. Make "hidden" ice creams, dipping a variety of flavours, and leaving everyone guessing.

SUGAR

Unless stated, sugar in these recipes means refined white sugar (the kitchen table variety), but you can use castor sugar if you wish. Make sure sugar is dissolved completely in the mixture before churning or freezing.

Make sure you taste the chilled mixture before freezing it. Cold mixtures support a much sharper flavour as freezing tends to diminish the true flavour. So, if a mixture tastes right before freezing, it will be disappointing after.

THE ICE CREAM CHURN AND HOW IT WORKS

If you are buying (or already own) a bench-top ice cream churn, it is important to understand how it operates.

Churning throws some of the mixture against the sides of the canister which is immersed in ice and salt to lower the temperature of the mixture as it solidifies. The dasher scrapes the sides of the canister which mixes the solidifying ice cream with the rest of the mixture. This keeps the ice cream smooth, resulting in a creamy texture.

HOW TO MAKE ICE CREAMS AND FROZEN YOGHURTS IN AN ELECTRIC BENCH TOP ICE CREAM CHURN

1 Before proceeding read the manufacturer's operating instructions.
2 If you intend to ripen and store the newly made ice creams in the freezer, then turn the freezer to the coldest setting before you begin to make your ice cream.
3 Follow the recipes in this book up to the churning stage and chill the mixture in the refrigerator.
4 Chill the metal canister. (Before using the ice cream machine, always scald the inner canister with hot water to ensure the purity of the ice cream.)
5 Measure salt and prepare ice.
6 Pour the cold mixture into the chilled canister, keeping the level of the ice cream below the fill line so the ingredients will have ample room to expand during processing. Insert the dasher into the canister making sure its shaft engages in the recess in the bottom of the canister. Place the canister lid on top. Lower canister into ice bucket making sure the drive shaft matches up to the bottom of the canister.
7 Fill the ice bucket about a third full with ice cubes. Pour, or scatter a third of the measured quantity of salt over the ice cubes. Repeat these two layers twice more, ending with salt on top. The canister should revolve and the dasher remain stationary. When the mixture starts freezing and expanding, the motor may slow down. Processing should take between 30 and 50 minutes. Do not leave the machine to run longer than 50 minutes. At this stage the ice and salt will have lost most of its effectiveness and maximum freezing will have already taken place. With highly sweetened mixtures, like honey, and alcoholic ice cream mixtures, setting takes considerably longer. I have found it's not worth while to churn these mixtures.
8 Turn off the power and remove the plug before opening the ice cream canister.
9 The ice cream is now ready for ripening. This means "to mature" the ice cream, covered and air tight in the coldest part of the freezer. Ripening will take from one to two hours or longer depending on how efficient your freezer. But it can be ripened in the churn by removing the dasher and adding extra ice and salt to the ice bucket. If you do this, first pour off the water from the ice which has melted. Insulate it by covering with newspapers or towels. It will take about 30 minutes. Or scrape the ice cream into an ice cream container or a mould. (See notes on moulding page 13). When turning the ice cream out of the canister, be careful that salty water does not drip into the ice cream from the bottom of the canister.
10 In serving ice creams you'll find those which are set too hard are difficult to serve and rather tasteless. To improve the texture, rest approximately half to one hour in the lower part of the refrigerator, before serving. A mousse-like consistency is good with most ice creams.

And don't forget to lick the dasher! After all, it's the main prize at the end of churning.

WHAT YOU NEED

Ice and salt are needed for bench-top ice cream churns. The salt is cooking salt, then rock salt, which is the most commonly used for this purpose, and finally table salt or running salt which is the most expensive. It's easy to pour table salt straight from the packet, measuring as you go with a cup or tablespoon, though I prefer to use cooking salt. I pre-measure it into a cup measure and shake it into the churn from the cup. One part salt to seven parts ice cream is the ratio needed for successful ice cream churning.

Ice:

Bags of ice are expensive and time-consuming because you nearly always have to go out specially just to get the ice. For a 2 litre (8 cup) capacity churn you will need approximately 4 average-sized trays of ice and a quarter to one-third cup (4 tablespoons) of salt. I have worked with 6 tablespoons of salt in this sized churn. It certainly sets the ice cream faster, but the texture is more granular as a result.

Making ice:

Make as much ice as you have trays and space in the freezer, at least one day before you need it. As the ice sets, store in plastic bags in the freezer and re-fill ice trays immediately. I make 4 swiss roll tins of ice at night, turn them out in the morning into a large plastic bowl, place a tea towel over the top and smash the ice with a meat mallet. Any heavy object will do as long as it's not breakable. For me, making ice creams every day, day after day, this was an effective method. It took less than 5 minutes to prepare, and overnight I had enough ice to last me through several batches of ice cream making, at no extra cost. The smaller the ice the better area coverage you will obtain for your ice cream canister thereby churning more efficiently.

Don't leave the canister idle in the ice and salt mixture for more than a few seconds, or the mixture freezes to the sides of the canister and prevents it from turning freely.

HOW TO MAKE ICE CREAMS AND FROZEN YOGHURTS IN A MANUALLY OPERATED ICE CREAM CHURN

1 Before beginning read the manufacturer's instructions.
2 Follow the instructions for the electric bench-top ice cream churn up to stage 5.
3 Pour the cold mixture into the chilled canister, never filling it more than three quarters full to allow for expansion during churning. Insert the dasher aligning it as per the maker's instructions. Clamp the head down.
4 Fill the ice bucket one third full with ice cubes or crushed ice. Pour or scatter a third of the measured quantity of salt over the ice. Repeat these two layers twice more, ending with salt on top.
5 Begin turning the crank, slowly at first, for about 5 minutes. Turn only in the direction given in the manufacturer's instructions. After 5 minutes speed up a little, but never turn too vigorously, as it makes the ice cream granular. This is relatively easy, for if you do become tired, you may rest for a couple of minutes taking care the ice cream does not freeze on the sides of the canister as it makes cranking very difficult. It takes approximately 12-20 minutes for a hand-cranked ice cream. You should be able to feel the texture developing and you can see the ice cream through the clear lid, so you will know when it is ready for ripening.

6 Release the crank head, remove the canister and its lid and the dasher. Either scrape into an ice cream container, or a mould, rinsed out with cold water, or leave in the canister.
7 Finish with steps (9 and 10) on page 11.

There is a freezer-type of ice cream maker available in Australia. It is called a Sorbetiere. It is a small unit which fits into the average domestic deep freeze unit, or deep freeze compartment in a refrigerator.

It comes in several sizes. It usually has a smaller capacity than the ice cream "bucket" type churn I have discussed previously. It works on the same principle but uses the deep freeze as its chilling or setting medium, therefore it will only be as efficient as your freezer or freezer unit is cold. Ideally 0°C (32°F) or below. It is driven electrically by a small motor.

HOW TO USE A SORBETIERE

1 Turn the freezer to the coldest setting.
2 Read the manufacturer's instructions.
3 Make ice cream mixture according to the recipes in this book and chill.
   Chill the machine's ice cream canister too.
4 Pour the mixture into the chilled ice cream canister but never fill it more than three quarters full. Insert the dasher or dashers (some Sorbetieres have two). Clamp on the lid and place in the coldest part of the freezer. Carefully close the freezer door on the electric flex. Plug in. Turn on power and you will hear the Sorbetiere operating.
5 Try to avoid opening the freezer during the churning operation. You must maintain maximum coldness all the time. These churns can be left to complete the entire churning process. Sorbetieres cease churning when the mixture solidifies.
6 Turn off power. Unplug machine and remove from freezer. Either ripen in the Sorbetiere canister or scrape ice cream into an air-tight container, cover and freeze for approximately half an hour before serving.

THE FREEZE/BEAT METHOD

With mixtures which have a reasonably high fat content this method of making ice cream is more than adequate. However, with the leaner ice cream mixtures the freeze/beat method does not produce the smooth creamy texture which is obtained by churning. To obtain good results:

1. Turn the freezer or freezer compartment to the lowest temperature. Make mixture according to the recipe and chill it very thoroughly. Pour into an ice cream container or ice cream trays. Place, level, in the coldest part of the freezer and leave to set.

2. Chill a bowl large enough to hold the ice cream mixture and a rotary beater or the beater or beaters from an electric mixer. Everything must be very cold.

3. When the mixture is partially set, about one-third in from the edges, it is ready for beating. Scrape into chilled bowl and beat with chilled beater. Working quickly immediately return to the same container in which it was frozen. Cover and return to the same part of the freezer and leave undisturbed, to set and ripen.

The best containers to choose for this method of freezing are shallow metal containers. Metal is a good temperature conductor, therefore, the ice cream sets more quickly in it. Secondly, a shallow mixture will set more quickly than a deep one.

EQUIPMENT FOR 'HOME MAKING'

With today's modern kitchen equipment ice cream making is an enjoyable task, one to look forward to.

ELECTRIC:
AN ELECTRIC BENCH-TOP ice cream churn or SORBETIERE, is time saving. You can be busy with other tasks while the churns crank. (See how to use 11) They are available in the kitchen sections of most major department stores and in many cookware shops. Prices and capacities vary.

FOOD PROCESSORS or BLENDERS are versatile pieces of equipment, they do so many arduous preparation tasks in a minimum of time. Many of you will already own one of these, so use them for preparing ice cream mixtures, flavourings for yoghurt, and drinks.

MANUAL:
A CITRUS PRESS is better for extracting juice than a squeezer, because it also releases the essences in the skins. These are not essential to the ice creams, but they do intensify the flavours.

A FOOD MILL (Mouli) is a great asset if you don't have an electrical appliance for pureeing. It has the added advantage of sieving the food at the same time.

PESTLES AND MORTARS were used in the early days of ice cream making and horse-hair drum-shaped sieves. Some of you might have these items hidden away in a cupboard not knowing how useful they can be. A utensil which nearly everyone will have is a rotary beater. It's perfect for beating ice cream mixtures. If using the freeze/beat method, fork through the icy mixture then beat with the rotary beater. Another useful utensil is a potato masher. Use it for releasing the juices in fruits and mashing them when a puree is required. If a super-smooth texture is required then a sieve comes in useful, but don't sieve before using the masher, it's much easier once the fruits are crushed.

A moulded dessert is always a delight. MOULDS don't have to be fancy. Any mixing bowl or straight-sided vessel will do. Do beware of shapes with "shoulders" or ones with the tops being narrower than the base. No matter how hard you try, you will never unmould it in one piece.

Metal moulds give the best lines, they are usually sharper. Metal as well as being a good temperature conductor, is also slightly flexible, as is plastic. You can usually ease the mould away from the top of the ice cream by pulling it, and so release the vacuum caught between the bottom of the mould and the iced dessert.

Copper moulds must be tin-lined. If the tinning is anything but perfect there is danger of not only copper poisoning but also food discolouration. Beware of highly acidic ices like citrus and berries.

Glass moulds for ice creams are not a good choice, unless the glass is resistant to sudden changes of temperature. Dipping a mould direct from the freezer even into only warm water, could break it. It's almost impossible to release the vacuum from china and glass moulds. If you line a pudding basin with two long strips of foil, which are several thicknesses, and cross them over in the bottom of the basin leaving some to hold onto at the top, you have a chance of pulling the dessert out. But if you line the basin completely with foil or plastic, it wrinkles and marks the dessert. Unless you are covering it completely in cream, nuts, or suchlike, it spoils the aesthetic appeal. A knife or spatula can be used to smooth over any imperfections in the unmoulded ice. There are not many catastrophes which cannot be hidden under a cloak of whipped cream.

ICE CREAM SCOOP There are several sizes and types available. If you want professional looking ice cream cones and desserts, then you will need one of these.

SMOOTHY ICE CREAMS

These ice creams are all based on Smoothy , a mixture of milk and cream.

These recipes concentrate on a wide selection of flavours made with Smoothy, but without the addition of extra cream. As there is only approximately 12% of butter fat in Smoothy, these ice creams are rather 'lean'. This means they are excellent for dieters, except for those recipes where extra sugar is added, (a sugar substitute may be used in those recipes), and they are less expensive than those using added cream which you will find in the next section. Lean ice creams do not have the same smooth texture as their richer cousins. They are best eaten the day they are made, or within a few days of making.

FRESH FIG ICE CREAM
Serves 5

500 ml Smoothy
200 g fresh ripe figs, white
   or purple
½ cup sugar

Peel and chop figs roughly, cook slowly with sugar for 10 minutes, stirring from time to time to dissolve sugar and prevent catching. Puree in blender or food processor and cool. Add to Smoothy and mix well. Chill.

Either churn or set by the freeze/beat method. Cover and ripen in freezer for one to two hours, or until firm.

Garnish with chocolate curls or grated chocolate.

VANILLA ICE CREAM
Serves 8

1 litre Smoothy
1¼ cups sugar
vanilla flavouring

Mix all ingredients together and chill for one to two hours in the refrigerator. Either churn or set by the freeze/beat method and ripen, covered, in the freezer for two hours or until firm, before serving.

Photographed L. to R.:
Fresh Fig Ice Cream with Chocolate Curl
(see recipe this page).
Fresh Peach Ice Cream with Peanut Crackle
(see recipe page 16).

FRESH PEACH ICE CREAM
Serves 4-5

500 ml Smoothy
3 fresh peaches, white or yellow
½ cup sugar
½ teaspoon lemon juice
almond flavouring

Peel the peaches after dipping into boiling water. Cut into small pieces. Add the sugar and leave to mature at room temperature for two hours. Mix 1 cup of peaches and 1 cup of Smoothy and blend until smooth. Fold into the remaining peach pieces and Smoothy with the lemon juice and almond flavouring and chill. Either churn or set by the freeze/beat method. Cover and ripen for one to two hours in the freezer, or until firm.

Blending half the peaches helps to spread the flavour and adds colour, while the other half being left in pieces adds to the texture. Lemon juice is usually used with peaches to prevent them from browning. In this case, it is added later so that some discolouration takes place, because it is attractive in the ice cream.

FRESH PLUM ICE CREAM
Serves 6-8

500 ml Smoothy
6 large ripe plums
½ cup water
¼ cup sugar
vanilla flavouring
2 eggs
¼ cup extra sugar

Halve plums and remove stones. Stew plums in sugar and water, when tender add vanilla and leave to cool. Puree plums and juice in a blender or food processor, or work through a sieve.

Beat the eggs with the extra sugar, heat the Smoothy and pour onto the eggs. Return to the fire and stir until nearly boiling. Remove from the fire. Fold in the puree and vanilla and chill before churning or setting by the freeze/beat method. Cover and ripen one to two hours, or until firm.

BLACK OR RED CURRANT ICE CREAM
Serves 6-8

500 ml Smoothy
⅔ cup sugar
1 cup black or red currants
4 egg whites (optional)

This is a wonderful ice cream for all those lucky people with access to these lovely fruits.

Pull the fruit off the stalks and poach in a syrup made from ½ cup of water and 2 tablespoons of sugar. Simmer gently for 1 minute, drain and puree.

Sometimes you can find these currants in jars. All you do is drain off the juice, discard it and puree the currants. You may need slightly less sugar if using preserved fruits.

Mix the Smoothy, currant puree and sugar together and taste. Adjust the sugar if necessary. Leave to marinate and gather flavour for three to four hours before churning or setting by the freeze/beat method. If using the egg whites, beat to soft peaks and fold into the mixture 10 minutes before finishing churning or after beating in the freeze/beat method. Cover and ripen in the freezer for two hours, or until firm, before serving.

Serve in scoops and pour over a little iced vodka, cassis (black currant liqueur) or Kirsch at the table.

STRAWBERRY ICE CREAM
Serves 5

500 ml Smoothy
⅔ cup sugar
250 g fresh strawberries (or 2 punnets)
juice of 1 lemon
2 egg whites (optional)

Wipe strawberries with damp paper towel or wash if really dirty. Hull them and puree in a food processor or blender or mash with a potato peeler. Stir in the lemon juice, Smoothy and sugar. Leave to mature and gather flavours for three to four hours, stirring from time to time, to dissolve the sugar. Chill the mixture. Either churn or set by the freeze/beat method. If using egg whites, beat until soft peaks stage and fold into the ice cream 10 minutes before finishing churning or after beating, during the setting process of the freeze/beat method. Cover and ripen in freezer for one to two hours, or until firm.

CHOCOLATE SULTANA ICE CREAM
Serves 5-6

500 ml Smoothy
200 g cooking chocolate
½ cup sultanas

Break chocolate into squares and melt in a saucepan over hot water, with one cup of Smoothy. Stir from time to time with a wooden spoon until chocolate and Smoothy are well combined. Remove from the heat. Add remaining Smoothy and sultanas and leave to cool at room temperature so that sultanas soften and swell. Chill. Either churn or set by the freeze/beat method. If using the second method, when beating this ice cream it is only necessary to break up the mixture with a fork. If using beaters the sultanas will be crushed. Cover and ripen in the freezer for one to two hours, or until firm, before serving.

Serve in scoops topped with your favourite liqueur or iced Vodka.

PEANUT BUTTER ICE CREAM
Serves 5

500 ml Smoothy
½ cup crunchy peanut butter
½ cup sugar
vanilla flavouring

Mix Smoothy and peanut butter together in a saucepan using a whisk. Heat slowly until nearly boiling. Remove from heat and stir in sugar. Cool. Add vanilla and chill. Either churn or set by the freeze/beat method. Cover and ripen in the freezer for one to two hours, or until firm, before serving.

PRUNE ICE CREAM
Serves 5-6

12 prunes
500 ml Smoothy
4 tablespoons orange juice
⅓ cup soft brown sugar
pinch ground cloves

Stone prunes and chop medium-fine. Mix all ingredients together and chill. Either churn or set by the freeze/beat method. Cover and ripen in the freezer for one to two hours, or until firm, before serving.

If too firm leave in bottom of refrigerator for half an hour to soften slightly.

A dark, fruity ice cream which is delicious with toasted muesli scattered over each serving.

LEMON ICE CREAM
Serves 5

500 ml Smoothy
⅔-¾ cup sugar
juice of 3 lemons
rind of 1 lemon
2 egg whites (optional)

Using a vegetable peeler, pare the rind from 1 of the lemons, taking the rind only, no pith. Squeeze the lemons and mix with sugar. Stir in the Smoothy and add the rinds and taste. Add extra sugar if necessary. Leave to marinate with the rinds for two hours, stirring from time to time to dissolve the sugar.

Strain off the rinds and either churn or set by the freeze/beat method. If using the egg whites, beat to soft peaks and fold into the mixture 10 minutes before churning finishes, or during the setting process, after beating, if using the freeze/beat method. Cover and ripen in the freezer for one to two hours, or until firm.

BUTTERSCOTCH BRAZIL ICE CREAM
Serves 3-4

250 ml Smoothy
100 g Butterscotch Brazil nuts
⅓ cup sugar
vanilla flavouring

Crush nuts in a food processor, blender, or alternatively, place in a heavy plastic bag and crush with a heavy object. Stir into Smoothy with essence and sugar. Chill. Either churn or set by the freeze/beat method. Cover and ripen in the freezer one to two hours before serving, or until firm.

MORELLO CHERRY ICE CREAM
Serves 4-6

500 ml Smoothy
⅔ cup pitted Morello cherries, drained
½ cup syrup from cherries
2 tablespoons cherry brandy, optional
⅓ cup sugar
few drops red food colouring

Chop the cherries medium fine and stir all ingredients together, making sure the sugar is dissolved. Chill. Either churn or set by the freeze/beat method. Cover and ripen in the freezer until firm.

Photograph:
Morello Cherry Ice Cream (see recipe this page), in Brandy Snap Baskets (see recipe page 58).

This is a lovely reddish ice cream flecked with the dark red of the cherries. Scoops served in Brandy Snap Baskets (page 58) and topped with Chocolate Brandied Cherries (page 78) makes a grand finale to a good dinner.

EGGNOG ICE CREAM
Serves 4-6

1 cup Smoothy
4 eggs
1 cup milk
scant ½ cup sugar
vanilla flavouring
¼ teaspoon nutmeg

Beat the eggs to combine yolks and whites and stir in the other ingredients making sure the sugar is dissolved. Chill, churn or set by the freeze/beat method. Cover and ripen in the freezer for two hours, or until firm, before serving.

Sprinkle nutmeg over each serving of ice cream.

This ice cream is excellent served with mince pies, especially hot mince pies.

FRUIT MEDLEY ICE CREAM
Serves 5-6

500 ml Smoothy
200 g mixed dried fruits (sultanas, diced apricots, apples, peaches, pears and nectarines)
½ cup sugar
1 teaspoon vanilla flavouring
½ cup apricot brandy, optional

Soak fruits in half cup Smoothy for two hours or longer. Mix all ingredients together and chill. Either churn or set by the freeze/beat method. Cover and ripen in freezer for one to two hours, or until firm, before serving.

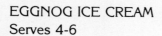

APRICOT PISTACHIO ICE CREAM
Serves 6-8

500 ml Smoothy
1¼ cups sugar
200 g dried apricots,
    chopped
3 tablespoons lemon juice
½ cup water
⅔ cup shelled pistachios
apricot brandy

Soak chopped apricots in lemon juice and water for 4 hours or overnight. Blanch pistachios in boiling water for 3 minutes, then slip off the skins between finger and thumb. Chop roughly. Stir all remaining ingredients except apricot brandy, into apricots and chill. Either churn or set by the freeze/beat method. Cover and ripen in the freezer for 2 hours, or until firm, before serving.

Serve with a tablespoon of apricot brandy spooned over each ice cream at the time of serving.

Pistachios are time consuming to shell and skin. It's best to do this menial task a day ahead.

APRICOT DELIGHT ICE CREAM
Serves 8

500 ml Smoothy
250 g dried apricots
½ cup water
¾ cup sugar
1 cup blanched almonds,
    toasted and chopped coarsely
3 tablespoons lemon juice
almond flavouring

Follow recipe as for Apricot Pistachio Ice Cream (see above).

CHRISTMAS MINCE ICE CREAM
Serves 6

500 ml Smoothy
300 g Christmas mince
3-4 tablespoons sugar
brandy, optional

Stir Christmas mince into Smoothy with optional brandy. Sweeten according to taste. Chill. Either churn or set by the freeze/beat method. Cover and ripen in the freezer for one to two hours.

If using a home made Christmas mince, it may well have brandy, rum or sherry in it. In such cases use the alcohol for the ice cream.

20

MAPLE SYRUP ICE CREAM
Serves 6

500 ml Smoothy
½ cup maple syrup
1 cup pecans or walnut pieces

Mix all ingredients together and chill for several hours. Either churn or set by the freeze/beat method. Cover and ripen in the freezer for one to two hours, or until firm, before serving.

PUMPKIN PIE ICE CREAM
Serves 8

500 ml Smoothy
500 g pumpkin
⅔ cup brown sugar
1 egg
½ teaspoon salt
1 teaspoon cinnamon
½ teaspoon ginger
¼ teaspoon cloves
grated nutmeg

Scoop out the pumpkin seeds, skin and cut into pieces. Bring to the boil in a little cold water and simmer until tender. Drain and mash. When cooled, mix with all the other ingredients, chill and churn or set by the freeze/beat method. Ripen, covered, in the freezer for 1-2 hours, or until firm, before serving with additional nutmeg sprinkled over the top.

As easy as pie, this ice cream is just like the American pumpkin pie — only frozen. It's unusual, different, and cheap!

DRIED APRICOT ICE CREAM
Serves 6

500 ml Smoothy
1¼ cups sugar
200 g dried apricots, chopped
3 tablespoons lemon juice
½ cup water

Soak chopped apricots in lemon juice and water for four hours or overnight.

Stir Smoothy and sugar into apricots and chill. Churn or set by the freeze/beat method, until a firm ice cream is reached. Cover and ripen in the freezer for two hours, or until firm.

Delicious served with chocolate sauce, and very good scooped into meringue cases.

Large pieces of hard frozen fruit are unpleasant in ice cream, so remember to chop the fruits fairly finely.

ORANGE ICE CREAM
Serves 4-5

500 ml Smoothy
⅔ cup sugar
3 beautiful oranges
2 egg whites (optional)

Using a vegetable peeler, pare the rind (skin only, no pith) off the oranges. Squeeze the oranges. Mix juice, rind and sugar with Smoothy and leave to marinate for a few hours. Stir from time to time to dissolve the sugar.

Chill the mixture. Strain to remove the rinds and set by churning, or by the freeze/beat method. If you'd like a lighter ice cream, beat the egg whites to soft peaks, and fold into the mixture 10 minutes before the end of churning or after beating half way through the setting of the freeze/beat method.

Cover and leave to ripen in the freezer for several hours before serving.

CHERRY RIPE ICE CREAM
Serves 4-6

500 ml Smoothy
1 cup desiccated coconut
½ cup sugar
2 teaspoons coconut essence
60 g red glace cherries, chopped
125 g dark chocolate, grated

Heat coconut in Smoothy on very low heat for 10 minutes. Do not boil. Stir in sugar. Cool. When cold, add coconut essence and chocolate. Churn or set by the freeze/beat method. When nearly set, fold in cherries, cover and leave to ripen in the freezer for two hours.

COCONUT ROUGH ICE CREAM
Serves 6

500 ml Smoothy
1 cup desiccated coconut
½ cup sugar
125 g dark chocolate, grated
coconut flavouring

Heat Smoothy with coconut for 10 minutes over a low heat. Stir in sugar and cool.

When cold, stir in essence and chocolate and chill. Churn or set by the freeze/beat method. Cover and ripen in the freezer for two hours.

Serve scooped into glass dishes with or without chocolate sauce.

FROZEN COCONUT ICE
Serves 4

500 ml Smoothy
1 cup desiccated coconut
½ cup sugar
coconut flavouring
red food colouring
CocoRibe liqueur

Heat coconut in the Smoothy on very low for 10 minutes. Cool the mixture and when cold, add the other ingredients except the food colouring. Divide the mixture into two, colour one half pink. Using the freeze/beat method pour into trays and leave to freeze until half set, then beat white half and spoon into a 20 cm x 20 cm square cake tin. Spread evenly over the tin, smooth over the top and freeze until firm. Meanwhile, beat the pink half and return to the freezer.

When the white half is set, beat the pink half a second time and spoon over the top of the white base. Smooth over and freeze overnight.

To serve, dip the tin in warm water and invert over a chopping board. With a sharp knife dipped in warm water, cut ice into squares and pile into a pretty glass bowl. At the moment of serving, pour over CocoRibe liqueur.

JAM ICE CREAM
Serves 4

500 ml Smoothy
2 tablespoons jam, jelly or
    conserve
food colouring, the
    colour of the jam (optional)

If using jelly, melt it gently and stir into Smoothy. If using conserve, and it is in chunky pieces, chop finely or puree before stirring into Smoothy. With jam, all you need to do is mash it with a fork and fold into Smoothy. Taste for sweetness and adjust with extra sugar or a little lemon juice. Add colouring and chill. Either churn or set by the freeze/beat method. Cover, and ripen in the freezer for one to two hours, or until firm, before serving.

Experiment with some of the following flavours — ginger marmalade or any marmalade makes a good and different ice cream. All the berry jams work wonderfully. And fig, plum, apricot, peach and pineapple. Try red currant or black currant ice creams made this way.

WHITE PEACH ICE CREAM
Serves 4-5

500 ml Smoothy
⅔ cup sugar
2-3 fresh white peaches
  (weighing 250 g approx.)
juice of ½ an orange
3 strips of orange rind
2 egg whites

Dip peaches into boiling water, skin and
chop flesh finely. Pour over the orange juice
to prevent browning. Stir into the Smoothy
with sugar and rind. Taste and add extra
sugar if needed. Leave to gather flavours for
two hours. Stir from time to time to dissolve
sugar. Chill. Either churn or set by the
freeze/beat method. Before setting beat egg
whites to soft peaks and fold into the ice
cream 10 minutes before churning is
finished. If using alternative method, fold in
the whipped egg whites after beating the ice
cream, half way through setting.

Cover and ripen in the freezer for one to two
hours, or until firm, before serving.

PEAR ICE CREAM
Serves 5

500 ml Smoothy
¾ cup sugar
4-5 canned or poached pear halves,
  drained
2 egg whites (optional)

Puree pears and mix with Smoothy and sugar. Leave to gather flavours for three to four hours, stirring from time to time to dissolve the sugar. Churn or set by the freeze/beat method. If you want a lighter ice cream, beat the egg whites to form soft peaks and fold into the mixture 10 minutes before finishing churning, or after beating during the setting in the freeze/beat method. Cover and ripen in the freezer for one to two hours before serving.

A refreshing and interesting ice cream, further enhanced by pouring over a little pear liqueur at serving time.

GINGER CHOCOLATE CHIP ICE CREAM
Serves 5-6

500 ml Smoothy
125 g dark chocolate, chopped
  finely
½ cup preserved ginger in syrup
1 cup sugar

Strain the syrup from the ginger and reserve it. Chop the ginger into very fine pieces. A food processor will chop it efficiently and finely in a few seconds. Mix all the ingredients together, including the syrup and either churn or set by the freeze/beat method.

Cover and ripen in the freezer for one to two hours, or until firm, before serving in scoops with a little biscuit, like Langues de Chat (see page 82), or serving with bananas.

Photograph:
Ginger Banana Split (see recipe page 78).

SMOOTHY ICE CREAMS WITH CREAM

Smoothy Ice Creams with additional cream, are smoother and richer than those made without, as in the previous section.

Smoothy and cream mixed with flavourings, like fruits, nuts, essences and liqueurs, sweetening and sometimes eggs, make an ideal base from which to create ice cream.

There are lots of flavours and ideas to experiment with in this section. Try some of these recipes and then create some of your own.

SMOOTHY VANILLA ICE CREAM
Serves 12

1 litre Smoothy
1⅓ cups sugar
600 ml thickened cream
vanilla flavouring
⅓ teaspoon salt

Mix all ingredients together and chill, covered in the refrigerator, for one to two hours. Either churn or set by the freeze/beat method. Cover and ripen in the freezer for two hours, or until firm, before serving.

RICH VANILLA ICE CREAM
Serves 14

1 litre Smoothy
1⅓ cups sugar
600 ml thickened cream
vanilla flavouring
4 egg yolks
⅓ teaspoon salt

Whisk yolks and sugar together, stir in essence, salt and Smoothy, and finally cream. Chill for one to two hours in the refrigerator. Either churn or set by the freeze/beat method and ripen, covered, in the freezer for two hours, or until firm, before serving.

CANNED FRUIT ICE CREAM
Serves 6-7

500 ml Smoothy
1 x 425 g can fruit of your choice, or fruit puree
sugar to taste
lemon or orange juice to taste
150 ml thickened cream, optional

If fruit is in a highly-sweetened syrup drain it off reserving fruit. Then puree fruit and stir in Smoothy. Taste and add sugar if necessary and citrus juices. Whip the cream until it forms soft peaks. Fold into mixture and chill. Either churn or set by the freeze/beat method. Cover and ripen in the freezer for one to two hours before serving.

This recipe makes quick and easy ice creams from canned mangoes, Kiwi fruits, pineapple, gooseberries, etc. It's great fun experimenting with all the canned fruits and purees available today. It also means you can be enjoying ice creams from fruits which are out of season.

CHOCOLATE CHESTNUT ICE CREAM
Serves 8-9

500 ml Smoothy
1 x 450 g can (approx.) sweetened chestnut puree
100 g cooking chocolate
150 ml thickened cream
2 tablespoons rum

Break chocolate into squares. Sieve the puree. Soften puree over a low heat with the chocolate and 1 cup of Smoothy. When the chocolate has melted, whisk the mixture until smooth. Add the remaining Smoothy. Whisk again. Remove from the heat and cool. Beat the cream until it forms soft peaks and fold in rum. Fold cream mixture into cold chestnut mixture. Either churn or set by the freeze/beat method. Cover and ripen in the freezer for one to two hours, or until firm, before serving.

If you have unsweetened puree then you will need to add castor sugar to taste, to this recipe. It should be beaten with the cream. Chestnut puree comes in various sizes between 438 g and 500 g.

It is wise to beat the cream while it is cold and without the rum. Sometimes, cream is inclined to curdle when the flavouring is added before it is thickened.

APRICOT LIQUEUR ICE CREAM
Serves 8-9

500 ml Smoothy
4 egg yolks
60 glace apricots
30 g slivered almonds, toasted
½ cup sugar
300 ml thickened cream
3 tablespoons apricot brandy
vanilla flavouring

Chop apricots finely and soak in apricot brandy for two hours. Whisk yolks and sugar until pale and frothy. Heat Smoothy and pour over yolks, return to heat and cook stirring all the time until the custard thickens. Remove from heat, stir in vanilla and cool with a circle of greaseproof paper directly on top of the custard. When cooled, fold in apricots, brandy and cream. Chill. Set in a churn, or by the freeze/beat method. Fold in the almonds just before setting point. Cover and ripen in the freezer one to two hours.

Serve in individual stemmed glasses with a little apricot brandy poured over the top.

CASSIS ICE CREAM
Serves 10

500 ml Smoothy
1 cup preserved blackcurrants, drained
4 egg yolks
⅓ cup sugar, or to taste
300 ml thickened cream
3 tablespoons Cassis (blackcurrant liqueur)

Whisk yolks and sugar until pale and frothy. Heat Smoothy and pour over yolks. Return to fire and cook stirring all the time until the custard thickens. Remove from heat. Stir in blackcurrants and liqueur. Cool with a circle of greaseproof paper directly on top of the custard. When quite cold, fold in cream. Set in a churn or by the freeze/beat method. Cover and ripen in the freezer for one hour, or until firm. Before serving rest in the bottom of the refrigerator for half an hour.

COFFEE PRALINE ICE CREAM
Serves 5-6

500 ml Smoothy
150 ml thickened cream
2 tablespoons instant coffee powder
⅔ cup sugar
¾ cup praline powder, hazelnut, almond, or walnut

Mix all ingredients together (see Praline powder page 78) and chill. Either churn or set by the freeze/beat method. Pour into a 750 ml (3 cup) mould which has been rinsed out with cold water, cover and freeze a further two hours, or until firm.

Invert the mould, after dipping in warm water, over a serving plate and serve with either a chocolate sauce or a coffee-based liqueur.

CHOCOLATE ICE CREAM
Serves 6

500 ml Smoothy
250 g cooking chocolate
⅓ cup icing sugar, sifted
150 ml thickened cream

Break chocolate into small pieces and melt over hot water with Smoothy and icing sugar, stirring with a wooden spoon. Cool. When quite cold, fold in cream. Chill. Either churn or set by the freeze/beat method. Cover and ripen in the freezer for one to two hours, or until firm, before serving.

APPLE PIE ICE CREAM
Serves 6

500 ml Smoothy
¾ cup bought apple sauce
sugar, optional
150 ml thickened cream
pinch ground cloves
⅛ teaspoon cinnamon
½ teaspoon green food colouring

Mix all ingredients together and chill. Either churn or set by the freeze/beat method. Cover and ripen in the freezer for one hour, or until firm. Before serving, rest in the bottom of the refrigerator if too firm.

Apple sauces vary in sweetness. I love this recipe without any sugar. For a sweeter flavour, add the sugar.

PISTACHIO ICE CREAM
Serves 5-6

500 ml Smoothy
150 ml thickened cream
⅔ cup sugar
150 g pistachios
green food colouring, optional

Skin pistachios by blanching in boiling water for several minutes or until the skins are loose. Slip off skins and dry pistachios. Chop coarsely.

Stir all ingredients together and taste. Adjust sugar if necessary. Leave, refrigerated for three to four hours to gather flavours before either, churning or setting by the freeze/beat method. Cover, and ripe for one to two hours, or until firm, in the freezer.

RHUBARB WALNUT ICE CREAM
Serves 8

4 medium sticks rhubarb
150 ml water
¼ cup sugar
500 ml Smoothy
2 x 60 g eggs
250 ml thickened cream
½ cup walnut pieces, chopped
    coarsley

Wash and chop rhubarb into 4 cm lengths. Stew with water and sugar until tender and beginning to break up. Cool. Make a custard by beating the eggs and sugar until pale and light. Heat the Smoothy until nearly boiling. Pour over the eggs whisking all the time. Return to the heat and thicken stirring constantly until mixture coats the back of a wooden spoon. Take from the fire, and leave to cool covered with a circle of greaseproof paper directly on top of the custard.

Beat the cream. When the custard is quite cold, fold in the rhubarb and cream and either churn or set by the freeze/beat method. If churning, fold in the walnuts during the last 10 minutes of churning. If using freeze/beat method, fold in the walnuts after beating the ice cream half way through the setting process, return to the freezer and leave until set. Cover and ripen one to two hours, or until firm.

Excellent served with orange segments.

Photographed L. to R.
Rhubarb Walnut Ice Cream (see recipe this page).
Pistachio Ice Cream (see recipe this page).

HONEY ICE CREAM
Serves 4

500 ml Smoothy
5 tablespoons clear honey
150 ml thickened cream

Gently heat Smoothy and honey together until honey dissolves. Cool. Beat cream until it forms soft peaks. Fold into honey mixture. Pour into a freezer container, cover and freeze until beginning to set around the edges. Remove from container and beat, using a cold bowl and cold beaters. Return to container, cover and leave in the freezer until set. Preferably overnight.

Honey ice cream is delicious served with many fruity ice creams like apple pie, raspberry, chocolate, ginger, pear and many more. Topped with Praline (see page 78) or Jam Sauce (see page 73) it's a great treat.

Due to the extreme sweetness of the honey this is a difficult ice cream to set, therefore it is not worthwhile churning.

BLACK GRAPE ICE CREAM
Serves 5-6

1 cup Smoothy
400 g black grapes, on stalks
½ cup red wine
150 ml thickened cream
¼ cup sugar, approximately, or to taste

Wash and drain grapes. Pull from stalks and puree. A food mill gives the best result because it catches the seeds and skins. Otherwise, squash the grapes with a potato masher or fork and push through a sieve. Don't put them in a food processor or blender, unless you remove the seeds first. Stir sugar, red wine and Smoothy into the puree, in this order. Beat the cream until soft peaks form, and fold through the mixture. Chill. Either churn or set by the Freeze/beat method. Cover and ripen in the freezer for one to two hours, or until firm, before serving.

This is an unusual ice cream deserving appreciative guests. Try serving it scooped into Tulipe Biscuits (see page 59).

If using a sweet red wine, you will need to add only a little sugar, or none at all.

ROCKY ROAD ICE CREAM
Serves 6

500 ml Smoothy
300 ml thickened cream
⅓ cup sugar
vanilla flavouring
½ cup choc bits
½ cup chopped almonds or walnuts
1 cup chopped marshmallows, pink and white

Mix Smoothy, cream, sugar and vanilla together and chill. Either churn or set by the freeze/beat method. When nearly set, fold in almonds, choc bits and marshmallows, snipped into small pieces with a pair of scissors. Set by the freeze/beat method, cover and ripen one hour, or until firm.

Delicious served with Hot Fudge Sauce (see page 75).

This ice cream has too many chunky pieces in it to churn satisfactorily.

ROCKY ROAD AND RAISIN ICE CREAM
Serves 6-8

Make as for Rocky Road Ice Cream (see above), but add ½ cup raisins plumped in 2 tablespoons of whisky or brandy.

LEMONY GINGER ICE CREAM
Serves 6

500 ml Smoothy
150 ml thickened cream
½ cup sugar, or more to taste
½ cup preserved ginger in syrup
1 tablespoon lemon juice
1 dessertspoon finely grated lemon rind.

Drain the syrup from the ginger and reserve it. Finely chop the ginger, then mix all the ingredients together, with the syrup. Taste and add extra sugar if necessary. Chill. Churn or set by the freeze/beat method.

Cover and freeze a further one to two hours, or until firm.

This is a refreshing ice cream after a rich or heavy meal. Wafer biscuits are a good accompaniment.

A food processor fitted with the metal blade is the quickest way to chop the ginger in this recipe, and it is not necessary to drain the syrup from the ginger to do this.

KAHLUA HAZELNUT PRALINE ICE CREAM
Serves 6

500 ml Smoothy
¾ cup hazelnut praline
150 ml thickened cream
3 tablespoons Kahlua liqueur

Mix all ingredients together (see Praline page 78) and chill. Either churn or set by the freeze/beat method. Cover and ripen in the freezer for two hours, or until firm, before serving.

At serving time, pour a little extra Kahlua over the ice cream and garnish each plate with a freshly picked flower.

QUINCE ICE CREAM
Serves 6-8

1-2 medium-large quinces
water to cover
¼ cup sugar
vanilla flavouring
500 ml Smoothy
½ cup sugar
2 eggs
300 ml thickened cream

Peel the quinces, remove the cores and cut into quarters then eighths. Cover with water, add the ¼ cup sugar and simmer for 45 minutes or until tender and a good deep salmon red. (They deepen in colour as they cook.) Cool and blend to a puree, which must measure 1¾ cups. If not, add water to make up to 1¾ cups. Heat the Smoothy until nearly boiling. Whisk the eggs and sugar together and pour over the hot Smoothy. Return to the cooker and stirring all the time, cook until nearly boiling. Take off the heat, stir in the quince puree and stand until cold. Either churn or set by the freeze/beat method. Cover and ripen until firm.

This ice cream is fairly heavy due to the texture of the fruit. It can be lightened by whisking 2 egg whites until they form soft peaks, and folding into the mixture during the last 15 minutes of churning or after beating, during the half set stage of using the freeze/beat method.

Because of the coarse texture of quinces, like pears, don't expect this ice cream to be very smooth. The flavour is so rewarding that it is worthwhile foregoing a super smooth texture.

CANTALOUP ICE CREAM
Serves 4-5

500 ml Smoothy
⅔ cup sugar
250 g ripe, well perfumed cantaloup
150 ml thickened cream
juice of ½ an orange
2 egg whites (optional)
⅛ teaspoon ground ginger

It is absolutely futile to try to make this ice cream with anything other than a well-ripened, superb cantaloup. So wait for the season and choose wisely or you will be disappointed.

Halve the cantaloup, remove the seeds and skin it. Chop into cubes and puree in a food processor or blender. Failing that, dice very finely and place in a bowl. Sprinkle over the ginger, orange juice, and sugar and leave half an hour to bring out the flavours. Stir in the Smoothy and leave to gather flavours for two hours, stirring from time to time to dissolve the sugar. Whip cream until it forms soft peaks and fold into mixture. Chill.

Either churn or set by the freeze/beat method. If using the egg whites, first beat them to soft peaks and fold into the nearly set mixture, 10 minutes before the end of churning, or after beating during the freeze/beat process.

Cover and ripen in the freezer, for one to two hours, or until firm.

IRISH MIST CREAM
Serves 10

1 litre Smoothy
300 ml thickened cream
4 tablespoons instant coffee powder
1¼ cups sugar
⅔ cup Irish Mist liqueur

Dissolve instant coffee in a little Smoothy and mix in all remaining ingredients. Chill. Either churn or set by the freeze/beat method. Cover ice cream with foil and ripen in the freezer for 2-2½ hours, or until firm, before serving.

Note: Setting will take longer with a liqueur base mixture. The alcohol slows down the freezing process.

Memories of Irish Whisky arise from this wonderfully smooth ice cream. Serve with Raisin Sauce (see page 71).

ICE CREAM FILLED CITRUS FRUITS

These have been popular in France for a long time and are available in most supermarkets and food shops.

The range is limitless. Try black currant ice cream in lemon, orange or grapefruit skins. All the berry ice creams are successful presented this way, and they can be made ahead. For a lighter, more refreshing result, heap sherbet into citrus skins.

Photographed L. to R.
Orange Oranges (see recipe page 32).
Lemon Lemons (see recipe this page).

LEMON LEMONS
Serves 10-12

10-12 large lemons with good skins
rind of 2 lemons, finely grated or
   shredded
1 cup Smoothy
$\frac{2}{3}$ cup sugar
600 ml thickened cream
5 egg yolks
7 tablespoons lemon juice

Proceed as for Orange Oranges (see page 32).

31

ORANGE ORANGES
Serves 10-12

1 cup Smoothy
10-12 medium navel oranges, with
    good skins
rind of 2 extra oranges, finely grated
    or shredded
½ cup sugar
600 ml thickened cream
5 egg yolks
5 tablespoons orange juice, from the
    oranges
2 tablespoons lemon juice
orange food colouring

Preparing orange skins:
Cut off the top ⅓ (stem end) of each of the
large navels. Using a grapefruit knife, scrape
out the flesh over a bowl being careful not to
damage the skins and reserve it. Wet the
skins and place in the freezer to frost. You
can frost the 'lids' too if you like, but they
must be emptied of all flesh first.

Making the ice cream:
Place Smoothy, 1½ cups of the cream,
orange rind and sugar into a saucepan.
Bring to a simmer, stirring from time to time.
Beat yolks in a large bowl, pour over the hot
Smoothy mixture, beating all the time.
Return to the pan, and cook over low heat,
stirring all the time, until the mixture coats
the back of a wooden spoon.

Place a circle of greaseproof paper directly
over the top of the custard to prevent a skin
from forming. When the custard is quite
cold, stir in orange juice obtained from
straining the flesh from the skins. Stir in the
lemon juice. Whip remaining cream until
soft peaks form and fold into custard. Colour
to a pretty orange with food colouring.
Churn, or set by the freeze/beat method.

Spoon ice cream into the prepared orange
skins, packing it in tightly. Fill generously,
high above the skins. Place the lids on top of
the ice cream and return to the freezer,
individually wrapped in plastic until ready to
serve. If storing for long (three weeks is the
recommended maximum time), keep
airtight in a plastic bag as well as plastic
wrapped.

Defrost slightly for half an hour before
serving, in the lower part of the refrigerator.

A citrus press will obtain maximum flavour
from the essences in the skins, as well as
pressing out the juices. Extra oranges are
needed if using this method and the juices
from the shells can be served at breakfast.

BERRY ICE CREAM

Follow the recipe for Strawberry Ice Cream
(see page 16) but substitute any berry fruit
which appeals to you. Blackberries,
raspberries, loganberries, youngberries are
all excellent in ice cream. Taste the mixture
before setting. Since some berries are
sweeter than others and some have more
acid, you may need to add or subtract sugar
or lemon juice. Remember that cold food,
like ice cream, supports a stronger flavour
than a warm food. That is, once it is frozen
the flavours don't come through as strongly
as when you are making it.

BLACKBERRY ICE CREAM
Serves 4-5

500 ml Smoothy
1 cup fresh blackberries
½ cup sugar

Crush the blackberries (a potato masher is
efficient) and stir in the sugar. Taste and add
more sugar if the berries are a little tart. Leave
to stand for several hours to develop the
flavours, then mix in the Smoothy and churn
or set by the freeze/beat method.

Cover and ripen in the freezer for one to two
hours, or until firm.

This very easy recipe is adaptable to
strawberries, raspberries, boysenberries,
youngberries and loganberries.

Because it is a lean ice cream, with no extra
cream or eggs added, a better result is
obtained from churning.

FROZEN BOYSENBERRY ICE CREAM
Serves 6-8

500 ml Smoothy
300 g frozen boysenberries,
    thawed
½ cup sugar
few grains salt
vanilla flavouring
1 teaspoon lemon juice

Puree boysenberries using a food processor,
blender, or potato masher. Fold into
Smoothy with remaining ingredients and
chill. Either churn or set by the freeze/beat
method. Cover and ripen in the freezer for
one to two hours, or until firm, before
serving. If too firm, leave half an hour in the
bottom of the refrigerator to soften slightly.

CREAM ICE CREAMS

Ice creams made with cream as the major ingredient are very rich. Therefore, allow for smaller servings. They do not require churning and so are amongst the simplest and quickest ice creams to make. You will be amazed at the smooth results.

VICTORIAN BROWN BREAD ICE CREAM
Serves 5

½ cup Smoothy
300 ml thickened cream
1½ cups fresh brown
   breadcrumbs
2 egg yolks
⅓ cup castor sugar
1 tablespoon Maraschino

Beat the yolks and sugar together in a medium-sized bowl until pale and light. Heat Smoothy in a medium-sized saucepan and when very hot, but not boiling, pour slowly over the yolk mixture, whisking all the time. Return mixture to the saucepan and cook the custard over a low heat, stirring constantly. Watch very carefully that the mixture does not boil or it will curdle. As soon as the mixture lightly coats the back of a wooden spoon, remove from the heat and pour over the breadcrumbs. Leave to cool.

Beat the cream until it forms soft peaks and fold in the Maraschino. Fold into cold custard. Pour into a serving dish. 2½-3 cup size. Cover and ripen in the freezer.

Commercially prepared breadcrumbs are not nearly as successful as fresh breadcrumbs in this ice cream.

CHERRY BROWN BREAD ICE CREAM
Serves 6

Victorian Brown Bread Ice Cream
cherry conserve

Make Victorian Brown Bread Ice Cream (see above). Just before setting, swirl in 1 cup of cherry conserve using a fork. Leave a pretty marbled affect.

TEA ICE CREAM
Serves 4

300 ml milk
1 small piece vanilla bean
2 tablespoons Indian tea, dry
⅓ cup castor sugar
1 egg
150 ml thickened cream

Slowly heat milk and vanilla bean until boiling. Pour over tea. Cover and leave to infuse for five minutes. Beat eggs and sugar together until pale and the mixture makes ribbons. Strain milk into the egg mixture. Pour into a saucepan and cook over a low heat until the custard coats the back of a wooden spoon. Cool with a circle of greaseproof paper placed directly on top of the custard. Whip the cream until soft peaks form and fold into the cold-tea-flavoured custard. Turn into a container, cover and freeze until firm.

This old Victorian recipe which is absolutely delicious though rich, should be accompanied by little biscuits like macaroons, meringues, Langues de Chat. (See page 82).

FRESH KIWI ICE CREAM
Serves 5-6

300 ml thickened cream
6 ripe Kiwi fruit
½ cup sugar
2 teaspoons cornflour
1 tablespoon water

Cut fruit in halves and scoop out the flesh with a teaspoon. Puree in a food processor, blender, or food mill. Otherwise mash with a potato masher or a fork to a smooth puree. It should measure approximately 2 cups. Pour ⅔ cup of the puree into a small pan, add the sugar and heat gently until simmering. Mix the cornflour and water together and stir into the hot puree. Cook over low heat, stirring with a wooden spoon until the puree thickens. Continue to cook a further two minutes. Remove from heat and cool. Beat cream until it forms soft peaks and fold in remaining fresh puree. When the cooked puree is quite cold, fold into the cream mixture. Turn into a container or 750 ml (3 cup) mould, cover and ripen in the freezer until firm.

Note: If using a mould, remember to rinse out with cold water before pouring in ice cream.

FRESH RASPBERRY ICE CREAM
Serves 10

600 ml thickened cream
1 kg fresh raspberries
juice of 1-2 lemons, according to
    taste
1½ cups castor sugar

Beat cream until soft peaks form. Puree raspberries in a blender, food processor or by squashing with a potato masher. Fold in lemon juice and sugar. Stir into cream and adjust the flavour with extra lemon juice if necessary. Pour into a 1¼ litre (5 cup) wetted mould. Cover with foil and freeze until firm.

To serve, remove foil, dip into warm water and invert over serving plate. Shake the ice cream gently to loosen the mould, lift off mould, carefully remove, and return to the freezer to firm. Leave half an hour in the bottom of the refrigerator before serving.

This very rich fruity ice cream is lovely served with fresh berries.

Note: Don't wash raspberries as they retain water in their hollow centres which results in watery raspberries.

RUSSIAN RAISIN ICE CREAM
Serves 6-7

600 ml thickened cream
½ cup raisins
¼ cup brandy
2 slices glace pineapple, chopped
    finely
2 glace apricots, chopped finely
½ cup slivered almonds, toasted
vanilla flavouring
almond flavouring

Soak raisins in brandy for several hours or overnight. Beat cream until soft peaks form. Fold in all remaining ingredients. Pour into a 1 litre (4 cup) wetted mould, cover with foil and freeze until firm.

To serve, remove foil, dip the mould in warm water for a few seconds. Invert over a serving plate and shake out. If outside has melted from too much heat, return immediately to the freezer until firm. Rest half an hour in the bottom of the refrigerator before serving.

Delicious served with chocolate, orange, strawberry or Melba sauces. (See pages 72 and 73).

Note: It is not necessary to churn or beat this mixture during setting because it has such a rich base being made with cream.

GOOSEBERRY ICE CREAM
Serves 5

150 ml thickened cream
1 x 425 g can gooseberries
½ cup sugar

Puree the gooseberries and their juice with the sugar. Fold in the cream. Chill. Either churn or set by the freeze/beat method. Cover. Ripen in the freezer for one to two hours, or until firm, before serving.

MERINGUE ICE CREAM
Serves 8-10

600 ml thickened cream
50 g meringues
1-2 tablespoons icing sugar, or to
    taste
4 tablespoons brandy

Beat cream until if forms soft peaks. Break meringues into pieces about the size of peas and fold through cream with brandy and sugar. Pour into a 750 ml (6 cup) wetted mould, cover and freeze. When set, dip into warm water, invert onto a serving platter, garnish with crystallised violets and angelica. Serve after leaving for one to two hours on the bottom shelf of the refrigerator.

Don't let this ice get too soft, it will be too rich.

CUSTARD-BASED ICE CREAMS

These egg custard-based ices require a little more preparation since they need cooking first. However, the end result is so worthwhile, I know you will return to them time and time again.

And what do you do with all the left-over egg whites. There are several ways for using them which you'll find in the ice cream biscuit section.

DOUBLE ESPRESSO ICE CREAM
Makes 5-6 servings

1 quantity Rich Vanilla Ice Cream
3 teaspoons instant coffee powder
1¼ tablespoons finely ground
   espresso coffee beans

Make Rich Vanilla Ice Cream (see page 37), according to instructions, but heat coffee powder with Smoothy. Pour into a 750 ml (3 cup) wetted mould, cover and freeze.

When ice cream is half set, soften and fold in ground coffee beans. Cover and leave to set.

ZABAGLIONE ICE CREAM
Makes 5-6 servings

250 ml Smoothy
4 egg yolks
300 ml thickened cream
½ cup sugar
½ vanilla bean
⅓ cup marsala

Beat yolks and sugar until pale and frothy. Heat Smoothy with split vanilla bean in a medium-sized saucepan, and pour over yolks. Put on fire and cook stirring all the time until custard thickens and coats the back of a wooden spoon. Cool with a circle of greaseproof paper directly on top of the custard. Remove the vanilla bean, rinse and dry. Store in a glass jar for further use. Stir in the marsala and chill.

Beat the cream until it forms soft peaks, fold into custard and set in individual cups. Serve with whipped cream, grated chocolate and a maraschino cherry.

RICH CHOCOLATE ICE CREAM
Makes 5-6 servings

250 ml Smoothy
4 egg yolks
⅔ cup sugar, or to taste
300 ml thickened cream
5 tablespoons cocoa powder,
preferably unsweetened

Beat the sugar, cocoa and egg yolks together in a bowl. Heat the Smoothy in a medium-sized saucepan. Pour it over the yolks mixture return to cooker and stir until custard thickens, and coats the back of a wooden spoon. Stir all the time so it thickens evenly. Cover with greaseproof paper directly on top of the custard. Beat the cream until it forms soft peaks and fold into the cooled custard. Set custard in a wetted 750 ml (3 cup) mould in the freezer, until ready to serve.

FRESH PEACH ICE CREAM
Makes 7-8 servings

1 quantity Rich Vanilla Ice Cream
almond flavouring
2-3 very ripe beautiful peaches, white
   or yellow

Make Rich Vanilla Ice Cream (see page 37) according to instructions. Add almond flavouring in place of vanilla. Peel and chop peaches finely and fold into cooled mixture. Pour into a 1 litre (4 cup) wetted mould, cover and freeze.

STRAWBERRY ICE CREAM
Serves 7-8

1 quantity Rich Vanilla Ice Cream
125 g fresh strawberries

Wipe over strawberries with a damp cloth, hull them and slice. Make ice cream according to Rich Vanilla (see page 37) and fold strawberries into cooled mixture. Cover and freeze until set.

1-2 tablespoons of orange flavoured liqueur or Kirsch folded through the nearly set ice cream is a wonderful taste treat for a special occasion.

RICH VANILLA ICE CREAM
Makes 5-6 servings

250 ml Smoothy
4 egg yolks
⅔ cup sugar
300 ml thickened cream
vanilla flavouring

Beat the yolks and sugar until pale and frothy. Heat Smoothy in a medium-sized saucepan and pour over the yolks. Return to heat and stir constantly until custard thickens and coats the back of a wooden spoon. Add vanilla and leave to cool. Place a circle of greaseproof paper directly on top of the custard. Whip the cream until it forms soft peaks, and fold into the thoroughly cooled custard. Pour into a wetted 750 ml (3 cup) mould and leave to set.

Note: Because this ice cream is so rich, it is not necessary to beat half way through the setting period.

This Custard-Based Ice Cream is a neutral base which can be used in a number of ways and flavoured in many different ways as well.

If wanting to unmould this ice cream, first rinse the mould out with cold water, before pouring in the ice cream and freezing it.

To unmould: Dip the mould into tepid water, invert over a serving dish, and shake until the ice cream slips out. Return to the freezer to firm before garnishing and presenting.

This ice cream should be served semi-frozen so it has a mousse-like consistency.

WALNUT ICE CREAM
Makes 5-6 servings

250 ml Smoothy
4 egg yolks
½ cup sugar
300 ml thickened cream
⅓ cup shelled walnuts, or walnut
    pieces, very finely chopped

Beat yolks and sugar until pale and frothy, fold in the walnuts. Heat Smoothy in a medium sized saucepan until nearly boiling and pour over yolks. Return to heat and cook until thickened, stirring constantly. Cool with a circle of greaseproof paper placed directly over the top of the custard.

Whip the cream and fold into the custard. Pour into a wetted 750 ml (3 cup) mould. Cover and freeze until ready to serve.

Photograph:
Rich Vanilla Ice Cream with Fresh Fruits (see recipe this page).

APRICOT MACAROON ICE CREAM
Serves 8-9

1 quantity Rich Vanilla Ice Cream
1 cup canned apricot halves, drained
½ cup crushed macaroons
almond flavouring

Puree apricots. Make Rich Vanilla Ice Cream
(see page 37) according to the recipe. Fold
puree into custard as it cools. Add almond
flavouring to taste. Half an hour before ice
cream sets or at the beating stage of the
freeze/beat method fold in macaroons.
Cover and leave to set.

GIANDUIA
This ice cream with the strange sounding
name is a favourite of Italians.
Serves 6-7

1 quantity Rich Vanilla Ice Cream
⅓ cup cocoa powder
½ cup toasted chopped hazelnuts
extra sugar to taste

Make as for Rich Vanilla Ice Cream folding in
cocoa, hazelnuts and sugar if necessary, to
the egg yolk and sugar mixture. Finish the
same way as for Rich Vanilla Ice Cream, (see
page 37).

CHOCOLATE HAZELNUT ICE CREAM
Serves 6-7

Make as for Rich Chocolate Ice Cream (see
page 35) and add ½ cup skinned, toasted
and chopped hazelnuts to the egg yolk
mixture. Finish as in chocolate ice cream.

HAZELNUT ICE CREAM
Serves 5-6

Substitute ½ cup skinned and toasted
chopped hazelnuts for walnuts in the Walnut
Ice Cream recipe (see page 37). Make
according to Walnut Ice Cream.

WALNUT CHOCOLATE AND RAISIN ICE CREAM
Serves 8-9

1 quantity Rich Vanilla Ice Cream
½ cup walnut pieces, chopped
   coarsely
50 g cooking chocolate
½ cup raisins, chopped roughly

Break chocolate into squares and melt in a
small pan over hot water stirring from time to
time with a wooden spoon. Make Rich Vanilla
Ice Cream (see page 37) according to the
recipe, folding in the melted chocolate,
chopped walnuts and raisins with the sugar
and egg yolk mixture. Continue as for Rich
Vanilla Ice Cream.

ALMOND ICE CREAM
Serves 6-7

1 quantity Rich Vanilla Ice Cream
1 cup blanched almonds, toasted,
   and finely chopped
almond flavouring

Make Rich Vanilla Ice Cream (see page 37)
according to instructions mixing almonds
and flavouring with the egg yolks and sugar.
Finish in the same way as the other
custard-based ice creams.

LIQUEUR ICE CREAM
Serves 5-6

1 quantity Rich Vanilla Ice Cream
¼ cup liqueur of your choice

Prepare Rich Vanilla Ice Cream (see page 37)
according to the recipe. Fold liqueur into
nearly frozen ice cream approximately 10
minutes before churning is finished or after
beating at the half-set stage during the
freeze/beat method.

It is important to understand that alcohol
slows down the setting process of ice
creams, therefore it is sometimes easier to
add it at the end or even pour it over the ice
cream as it goes to the table.

RICH PISTACHIO ICE CREAM
Serves 5-6

250 ml Smoothy
4 egg yolks
2/3 cup sugar
300 ml thickened cream
100 g shelled pistachios
green food colouring

Pour boiling water over the pistachios and leave for 2-3 minutes. Test to see if the skins are loose. When ready, pour off the water and rub off the skins. Dry the pistachios on paper towel and chop medium fine in a food processor or blender or by hand.

Beat the yolks and sugar until light and frothy then stir in the pistachios. Heat the Smoothy and when nearly boiling, pour over the yolk mixture. Cook over a low heat until thickened, stirring all the time. Leave to cool with a circle of greaseproof paper directly on top of the custard.

Whip the cream and fold into the custard. Colour a pale green with a few drops of colouring. Cover and freeze until firm.

CROCCANTINO
Serves 6-7

1 quantity Rich Vanilla Ice Cream
150 g Amaretti biscuits, crushed
    finely

Make as for Gianduia Ice Cream (see page 38) mixing the crushed biscuits in with the egg yolks and sugar. Finish the same way.
Amaretti are small almond-flavoured Italian macaroon-type biscuits available at good supermarkets and continental delicatessens.

RICH MOCHA ICE CREAM
Serves 5-6

1 quantity Rich Chocolate Ice Cream
1 tablespoon finely ground espresso
    coffee beans

Make Rich Chocolate Ice Cream (see page 35) according to instructions. Pour into a wetted 750 ml (3 cups) mould. Cover and leave to set in the freezer. When half way through setting, soften and fold in ground coffee beans. Cover, return to freezer and set.

FLAMBEED FRUITS

Flambeed Fruits are one of the best accompaniments to ice cream, especially a rich creamy ice cream with a custard base. Any highly-perfumed ripe fruit in season is suitable for flambeeing. Basically, you need a fire, cooker, or table-top spirit burner, a shallow saute pan and an alcoholic liqueur. Experience will teach you how hot to have the heat, but a high flame is difficult and is not recommended when first learning about flambees. It is important that the alcohol content in the liqueur is burnt completely, otherwise your results will be poor. Rich Vanilla Ice Cream (see page 37) makes an ideal base for flambeed fruits.

FLAMBEED ORANGES
Serves 6

4 lovely ripe oranges
¼ cup castor sugar
Cointreau or other
    orange-flavoured liqueur

Peel the oranges using a very sharp knife removing the pith at the same time as the rind. Cut into segments in between the membranes. Place frying pan over heat and add sugar. When it is foaming pour on Cointreau and light. Add the orange segments, swirl around in the pan for a few seconds until the ingredients are well combined. By this time the flame will have died. Spoon very cold ice cream into the base of a large goblet or serving dish and pour over half the flamed orange. Return the frying pan to the fire and caramelise the remaining ingredients. Watch carefully that they do not burn. Add to the dish and serve immediately.

FLAMBEED STRAWBERRIES
Serves 6

200 g strawberries
¼ cup castor sugar
Cointreau, or other
    orange-flavoured liqueur

Wipe over strawberries with damp kitchen paper, and hull. Prepare flambe in the same manner as the orange recipe.

FLAMBEED FIGS
Serves 6

9-12 ripe well-perfumed figs
¼ cup castor sugar
3 tablespoons Kirsch
juice of half orange

Peel figs and cut in halves lengthwise if very large. Place frying pan on heat. Add sugar and allow to foam. Flame with half the Kirsch. Add the figs and orange juice. Turn over in the juices and flame with the remaining Kirsch. Prepare glass dishes or goblets with ice cream. Add half the flamed figs. Return the frying pan to the fire, caramelise the remaining ingredients and pour over the ice cream. Serve immediately.

PEACH FLAMBE
Serves 6

4 ripe well-perfumed peaches,
    white or yellow
¼ cup castor sugar
juice of half an orange
3 tablespoons Kirsch

Immerse peaches in boiling water for a few seconds. Remove the skin and stones, and cut into largish pieces. Proceed as for Flambeed Figs.

BANANA FLAMBE
Serves 6

¼ cup castor sugar
1 tablespoon butter
1 teaspoon cinnamon
3 tablespoons banana-flavoured
    liqueur, or Kirsch
4 ripe bananas
2 tablespoons rum

Peel bananas, cut crosswise into slices. Heat butter, sugar and cinnamon in saute pan until well combined and butter has melted, stirring all the time. Add banana liqueur and blend well. Add bananas and toss to coat thoroughly. Pour over rum, heat slightly and ignite. Shake pan gently until flame dies.
Prepare dishes with scoops of ice cream. Spoon over half the Flambeed Bananas, return the pan to the fire. Caramelise the remaining ingredients and spoon over the top. Serve at once.

TROPICAL ICE CREAM

These are fruit and nut ice creams for all those lucky enough to live in the tropics. I have made fresh fruit ice creams, especially for those fortunate enough to grow their own tropical fruits. However, for "southerners" I have devised a basic standard recipe using canned fruit.

No tropical section would be complete without pineapple. So do try it. It's on page 58 in the Grand Iced Desserts section with the other recipes which do not require churning.

BANANA ICE CREAM
Serves 4-6

500 ml Smoothy
½ cup sugar
3-4 ripe bananas, medium-sized
1½ tablespoons lemon juice
dash cinnamon, optional

Peel and mash bananas, then puree them in a food processor or blender with a cup of Smoothy. Or mash with a potato masher. Stir in remaining ingredients and chill. Either churn or set by the freeze/beat method. Cover and ripen in the freezer for 1-2 hours before serving.

A wonderful cheap and quick ice cream. It's nutritious and filling, and great with chocolate sauce.

FRESH MANGO ICE CREAM
Serves 5-6

500 ml Smoothy
2 large, ripe mangoes
sugar to taste
2 tablespoons lemon juice
almond flavouring

Peel mangoes and cut flesh away from seeds. Puree fruit. Beat puree and Smoothy together until thoroughly mixed. Stir in lemon juice and flavouring and taste. Add sugar if necessary. Chill. Either churn or set by the freeze/beat method. Cover and ripen in the freezer for one to two hours before serving.

Mangoes are rather fibrous, therefore if you want a super smooth ice cream — sieve the puree, then proceed with the recipe.

AVOCADO ICE CREAM
Serves 6-8

500 ml Smoothy
4 eggs
⅓-½ cup sugar
vanilla flavouring
2 medium-sized ripe avocadoes
2 tablespoons sugar, extra
    juice of 1 small lemon

Whisk the eggs and sugar until pale and frothy. Heat the Smoothy until almost boiling, pour slowly onto the eggs whisking all the time. Return to the saucepan and cook over low heat, stirring constantly until the custard thickens and coats the back of a wooden spoon. Stir in the vanilla and cool the custard with a circle of paper directly on top of it.

While the custard is cooling, cut the avocadoes in two, remove the stones and skins and immediately rub all over with lemon juice. Puree the flesh with the lemon juice and extra sugar in a food processor or blender or simply push through a nylon sieve using a wooden spoon. Fold into the cooled custard and churn or set by the freeze/beat method. Cover and ripen in the freezer until firm.

This is a very rich ice cream, with a wonderful green colour.

MACADAMIA NUT ICE CREAM
Serves 5-6

500 ml Smoothy
1½ cups shelled macadamia nuts
few grains salt
⅓ cup sugar
almond flavouring, optional

Chop the nuts very finely. A food processor, blender or nut mill are the most efficient. Otherwise, using a large board and a large knife, and lots of patience, chop the nuts and add to the Smoothy in a medium-sized saucepan and bring very slowly to the boil. Turn off the heat, put on lid and infuse for five minutes. Stir in sugar and salt, optional flavouring, and cool. Chill. Either churn or set by the freeze/beat method. Cover and ripen in the freezer for one to two hours before serving.

PAWPAW ICE CREAM
Serves 6-8

500 ml Smoothy
1 large, ripe pawpaw, weighing
   approximately 1 kg
½ cup sugar
1 tablespoon orange juice
2 tablespoons lemon juice
2 teaspoons gelatine, mixed with
   1 tablespoon water
300 ml thickened cream

Cut pawpaw in halves, scoop out seeds
and discard. Cut off skins and chop flesh
finely. Place in a heavy-based saucepan
over very low heat preferably with a
diffuser or asbestos mat. Heat gently for
about 30 minutes, covered, removing the
lid from time to time to stir. Dissolve
gelatine in hot water. Remove pawpaw
from heat and stir in citrus juices, gelatine
and sugar. Leave to cool. Beat cream
until it forms soft peaks and fold into
pawpaw mixture. Chill. Either churn or set
by the freeze/beat method. Cover and
ripen in the freezer for one to two hours
before serving.

GINGER ICE CREAM
Serves 4-5

500 ml Smoothy
½ cup ginger marmalade
⅓ cup Advocaat liqueur, optional

Mix all ingredients together and chill.
Either churn or set by the freeze/beat
method. Cover and ripen in the freezer for
one to two hours before serving.
The Advocaat, being high in alcohol will
slow down the freezing process. You can
serve this ice cream with Advocaat
spooned over the top.

PASSIONFRUIT ICE CREAM
Serves 5

500 ml Smoothy
2 x 125 g cans passionfruit pulp
2 tablespoons sugar, optional
2 tablespoons lemon juice,
   optional

Mix all ingredients together, taste and
adjust sugar and lemon juice if
necessary. Chill. Either churn or set by
the freeze/beat method. Cover and ripen
in the freezer for one to two hours.

CHILDREN'S PARTY ICE CREAM

Everyone loves a treat — especially children at party time. Why not make some of these ice cream party ideas and spoil your "littlies" both big and small? Better still, have them churn some ice creams and help with a favourite family chore.

LICORICE ICE CREAM
Serves 6

500 ml Smoothy
1½ cups licorice, finely chopped
1½ cups water

Place licorice and water together in a small saucepan and heat over a water bath, stirring from time to time with a wooden spoon, until licorice melts. Stir into Smoothy and chill. Either churn or set by the freeze/beat method. Cover and ripen in the freezer for 1-2 hours before serving.

PEPPERMINT CRISP ICE CREAM
Serves 5

500 ml Smoothy
6 x 30 g Peppermint Crisp bars
2 tablespoons sugar

Break Peppermint Crisp bars into a heavy plastic bag and crush with a rolling pin or heavy object. Mix all ingredients together and chill. Either churn or set by the freeze/beat method. Cover and ripen in the freezer for one to two hours.

PICNIC ICE CREAM
Serves 4

250 ml Smoothy
150 g Picnic Chocolate bars
⅓ cup sugar

Crush Picnic bars or chop finely using a food processor or blender, or chop on a board. Mix into Smoothy with sugar and chill. Either churn or set by the freeze/beat method. Cover and ripen in the freezer for one to two hours.

Serve in scoops with Chocolate sauce and extra Picnic bars crumbled over the top.

CHOCOLATE BANANA BOATS
Make 1 boat per child

ripe bananas
chocolate dipping mixture
scoops of ice cream of your choice
chopped nuts

Peel bananas, dip in lemon juice and place on foil-lined tray in the freezer until very cold but not frozen. Meanwhile prepare chocolate dipping mixture (see page 77). When ready, take bananas from the freezer and dip, one at a time, into the chocolate mixture. Completely submerge in the dipping mixture. Lift out, letting excess mixture run off banana. Leave to set on foil-covered tray.

Serve chocolate-coated-bananas in chilled long, shallow dishes. Top with scoops of ice cream and sprinkle with chopped nuts.

Serve immediately.

Note: On a hot day, this is not the easiest recipe to handle, so do try to keep your cool!

ICE CREAM TRAIN

ice cream (your child's favourite)
coloured Life Savers
licorice sticks

After processing the ice cream, set in rectangular cake tins lined with foil. Freeze overnight. When ready to make the train, unmould ice cream, carefully tearing away the foil. Cut into blocks. Rest on an oven tray covered in foil.

To form the engine: Stand one slice on the end of a block, to make the driver's platform. Place at one end of the tray. Use a licorice stick piece to form funnel.

To make carriages: Stand remaining blocks (carriages) behind engine, approximately ½ cm apart. Join them together with licorice stick pieces.

To make wheels: Place Life Savers at each corner of engine and carriages.

Place tray in freezer until ready to serve.

Note: This recipe is an easy one for a very simple train. You may like to decorate the train a little more, using your own creativity.

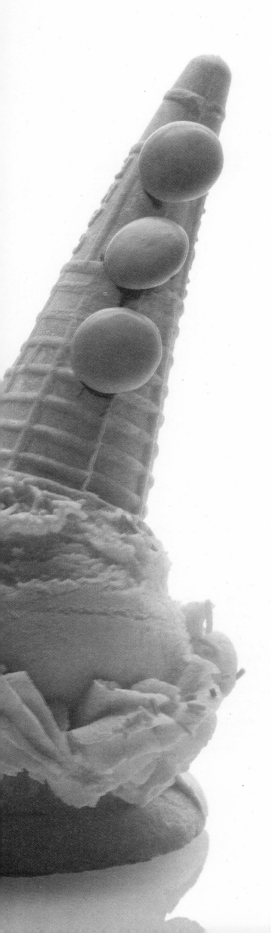

GOLLIWOG ICE CREAMS
Make 1 golliwog per child

scoops of vanilla, chocolate and
   strawberry ice cream
cornet ice cream cones
Smarties
chocolate nonpareilles
multi-coloured nonpareilles
desiccated coconut
Life Savers
coloured jubes
cooking chocolate, melted
glace icing (icing sugar mixed with
   thickened cream or Smoothy)
thickened cream, whipped

Cut through the cones where the cup joins
the cornet "handle" and place the cup
upside down on a baking tray covered with
foil.

Place a scoop of firm ice cream (see page
15, 25 and 16) on the inverted cup. Scatter
over chocolate nonpareilles or coconut to
make hair.

Using a small rose piping tube, pipe cream
around the base of the ice cream — or leave
plain.

To make the hats, dip the base of the cornet
into glace icing or melted chocolate, turning
to coat approximately 2.5 cm up the cone.
Then dip into chocolate nonpareilles, or
leave plain.

When the cornet is dry, decorate by sticking
a row of three smarties down one side using
melted chocolate or very stiff glace icing.

Place cornet on ice cream at a jaunty angle
and form faces with jubes, etc.

Place tray in the freezer until ready to serve.

45

FROSTED STRAWBERRY SUNDAE
Make 1 per child

strawberries
egg white
sugar
strawberry ice cream
strawberry sauce

Dip whole strawberries, unhulled, in egg white, shake off excess and roll in sugar. Place on a foil-covered plate and leave to set for a couple of hours. Scoop strawberry ice cream (see page 16) into stemmed glasses. Spoon over strawberry sauce (see page 72) and top with frosted strawberries.
Serve immediately.

COCONUT BANANA SPLIT
Make 1 per child

ripe bananas
vanilla ice cream
caramel sauce
desiccated coconut

Halve bananas lengthwise and place in a long shallow dish with scoops of ice cream, (see page 15). Spoon over caramel sauce (see page 75) and desiccated coconut.
Serve immediately.

PINEAPPLE CRUSH
Make 1 per child

scoops of vanilla ice cream
canned, crushed pineapple
pineapple topping
glace cherries

Place a scoop of ice cream (see page 15) in the bottom of each glass. Top with pineapple, then another scoop of ice cream. Pour pineapple topping over top and garnish with a cherry.
Serve immediately.

FRUIT SALAD DELIGHT
Make 1 per child

fruit salad
vanilla ice cream
strawberry or orange sauce
flaked almonds, toasted

Spoon fruit salad into party dishes, top with vanilla ice cream (see page 15) and pour over sauce, (see page 72). Scatter over toasted almonds and serve immediately.

HULA COOLER
Make 1 per child

strawberry ice cream
passionfruit pulp
kiwi fruit
orange sauce

Place scoops of strawberry ice cream (see page 16) into pretty dishes. Cover with passionfruit pulp and arrange slices of kiwi fruit around the edge. Serve with orange sauce, (see page 72).
Serve immediately.

KOOL MINT ICE CREAM
Makes 3 servings

250 ml Smoothy
100 g Kool Mints, plus extra for garnish
peppermint flavouring
½ teaspoon green colouring
1 teaspoon gelatine

Mix gelatine in 1 tablespoon hot water. Crush Kool Mints, either in a food processor, fitted with a metal blade, a blender, or alternatively, place in a heavy duty plastic bag and crush with a heavy object. Mix all ingredients together and chill. Either churn or set by the freeze/beat method. Cover and ripen in the freezer for one to two hours.

Serve with extra crushed Kool Mints scattered over the top.

Note: Kool Mints are extremely hard, so don't be tempted to crush them with a rolling pin. You will dent it irreparably.

MARSHMALLOW SURPRISE
Make 1 per child

scoops of vanilla and strawberry ice
   creams
strawberry sauce
pink and white marshmallows

Place a scoop of ice cream (see page 15 or
16) in the bottom of each glass. Spoon over
a little sauce (see page 72) and a few
chopped marshmallows. Top with another
scoop of ice cream. Pour sauce over top and
scatter over chopped marshmallows.
Note: The easiest way to cut marshmallows
is with a pair of scissors. If they stick to the
scissors, dip blades in icing sugar or flour.
Serve immediately.

FAVOURITE SUNDAE
Make 1 per child

vanilla ice cream
100's & 1000's
chocolate sauce

Toss scoops of vanilla ice cream (see page
15) into 100's & 1000's and serve with
chocolate sauce, (see page 75).
Serve immediately.

POPSICLES
Make 1 per child

ice cream, of your child's choice
icy pole sticks
paper cups

After choosing a suitable flavour, make
according to the recipe. Just before setting,
pour half a cup into paper cups set out on a
small tray — one which will fit in the freezer.
Freeze until almost set, place in the wooden
sticks so they stand upright, and leave until
ready to serve.

Carefully, cut away the paper cups and serve
popsicles as they are or dipped in chocolate
dipping mixture (see page 77) or into 100's
and 1000's or nonpareilles.

Any small containers, like foil patty pans or
small moulds or cups will suffice for
moulding popsicles.

These can be stored in plastic bags in the
freezer for several days.

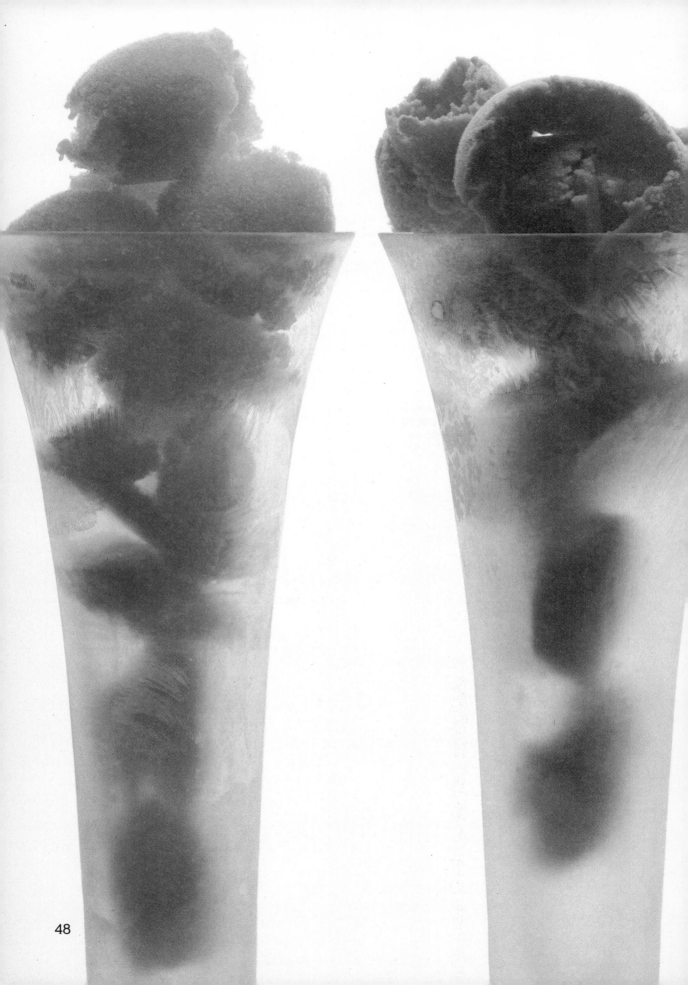

48

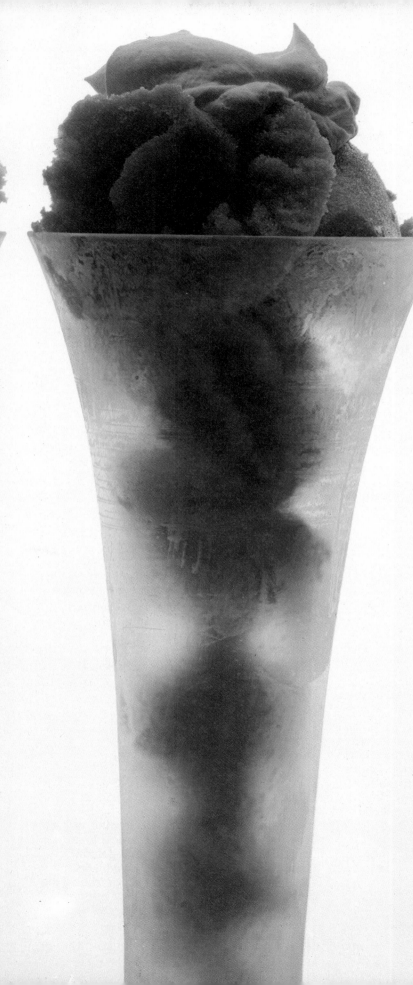

SKINNY SHERBETS

Sherbets, made with Skinny are easy and economical.

Because there is practically no fat, just 0.1%, these sherbets, like water-based sorbets, should be served the day they are made.

Keep sherbets fruity and not too sweet. They should be refreshing at all times, whether serving between courses as a palate cleanser or simply to end a meal on a tangy refreshing note. Too much sugar will spoil the effect and also make for a sticky result. Too much acidity makes the sherbet powdery. A happy medium has been devised for these recipes.

Sherbets look most attractive served in frosted long glasses. Place glasses in the freezer for an hour before spooning in the sherbet. The best way to serve a sherbet is to scrape a spoon across the top of the set mixture, letting it curl in the spoon. (see page 48). It helps to break up what can be a rather solid texture. If you find this tricky, soften the mixture slightly, then fork through the sherbet and serve at once, but it will melt more quickly this way. Sherbets are delicious with a spoonful of iced vodka poured over the top of each serving at the table.

SKINNY RASPBERRY SHERBET
Serves 5

500 ml Skinny
250 g raspberries, fresh or frozen
½ cup sugar
1 small lemon

Pare the rind from the lemon, and squeeze the juice. Puree raspberries and sieve them to give a smooth, seedless puree. Stir in sugar, juice, rind and Skinny. Leave to gather flavours for 3-4 hours. Strain out rind and chill the mixture. Either churn or set by the freeze/beat method. Ripen, covered in the freezer for 2 hours before serving.

Instead of raspberries, you may substitute blackberries, loganberries, youngberries, boysenberries or strawberries in this recipe.

Photographed L. to R.
Skinny Mandarine Sherbet (see recipe page 50).
Skinny Raspberry Sherbet (see recipe this page).
Espresso Sherbet with Chantilly Cream (see page 51).

SKINNY GRAPE SHERBET
Serves 8

500 ml Skinny
1 x 750 ml bottle natural grape
   juice, red or white
red or green food colouring
8 small clusters of grapes
1 egg white
castor sugar

Mix Skinny and grape juice together and colour red or green depending on which grape juice you use. Chill. Either churn or set by the freeze/beat method. Cover and ripen for 1-2 hours. Place long sherbet glasses in the freezer.

While the sherbet is ripening prepare the garnish. Break up egg white with a fork so it runs off the fork in a thin stream. Don't beat air into it. Dip clusters of grapes into egg white and drain off excess. Dredge in castor sugar and shake off excess. Leave on a foil lined tray in a warm place to dry.

Either spoon sherbet into frosted individual glasses or scrape using the side of a spoon, so the sherbet curls in the spoon. Top each serving with a cluster of frosted grapes.

Placing serving glasses in the freezer before serving, not only helps to prevent the sherbet from melting so quickly but also frosts the glasses, which is most attractive.

SKINNY MANDARINE SHERBET
Serves 5

500 ml Skinny
½ cup sugar
5-6 mandarines, medium sized
1 lemon
orange food colouring, optional

Using a vegetable peeler, pare the rind off the lemon, don't take any of the white pith, which is bitter.

Squeeze mandarines and lemon and strain out seeds. Stir juices and sugar together, add lemon rind and the mandarine skins. Stir in Skinny and colouring and leave to gather flavours for 3-4 hours, stirring from time to time to dissolve the sugar. Strain out the rinds and skins and chill.

Either churn or set by the freeze/beat method. Cover and ripen 1-2 hours before serving.

SKINNY LEMON SHERBET
Serves 5

500 ml Skinny
½ cup sugar
3 lemons

Using a vegetable peeler, pare the rind from 2 of the lemons, taking just the rind, no pith. Squeeze lemons, and strain out seeds. Mix with sugar and rinds. Stir in Skinny and leave to gather flavours for 3-4 hours, stirring from time to time to dissolve sugar. Chill. Set by churning or the freeze/beat method. Cover and ripen in the freezer for 2 hours before serving.

SKINNY ORANGE SHERBET
Serves 5

500 ml Skinny
½ cup frozen orange
   concentrate
2 teaspoons gelatine, softened
   in 3 tablespoons water

Heat Skinny in a small pan, stir in gelatine and heat until dissolved. Cool. When quite cold stir in thawed orange concentrate. Either churn or set by the freeze/beat method. Cover and ripen for approximately one hour.

ORANGE CURACAO SHERBET

Make as for Skinny Orange Sherbet, stirring in 2 teaspoons Orange Curacao at the same time as the orange concentrate.

This sherbet will take longer to set than orange sherbet because the alcohol slows down the freezing process.

SKINNY PASSION FRUIT SHERBET
Serves 5

500 ml Skinny
½ cup sugar
5 fresh passion fruit
juice of 1-2 lemons, depending
   on ripeness of passionfruit
1 tablespoon gelatine, softened
   with 4 tablespoons water

Squeeze the passion fruit, scraping out all the flesh, stir in sugar and lemon juice. Heat Skinny with gelatine until gelatine dissolves. Cool. When quite cold, stir in passion fruit and either churn or set by the freeze/beat method. Cover and ripen in the freezer for 1-2 hours before serving.

SKINNY PINEAPPLE SHERBET
Serves 5

250 ml Skinny
500 ml tinned pineapple juice
1 tablespoon gelatine, softened
  in 3 tablespoons water

Dissolve gelatine over hot water. Stir into pineapple juice and Skinny. Either churn or set by the freeze/beat method. Cover and ripen in the freezer for one to two hours before serving.

SKINNY COFFEE SHERBET
Serves 5

500 ml Skinny
2 tablespoons instant coffee powder
½-¾ cup sugar, to taste
2 teaspoons gelatine, softened
  in 3 tablespoons water

Dissolve gelatine over hot water. Stir half cup Skinny into coffee powder to mix well. Mix all ingredients together and chill. Either churn or set by the freeze/beat method. Cover and ripen in the freezer for half an hour before serving.

ESPRESSO SHERBET
Serves 5-6

500 ml Skinny
1 cup very strong black coffee,
  preferably espresso
sugar to taste
2 teaspoons gelatine, softened
  in 1 tablespoon water
Chantilly Cream

Dissolve gelatine in hot water. Mix all ingredients together and taste for sweetness. Chill. Either churn or set by the freeze/beat method. Cover and ripen in the freezer for one hour, or more if necessary, before serving.

Spoon into frosted long glasses and top with generous spoonfuls of Chantilly Cream (see page 72).

When served, each person should mix the Chantilly Cream into the sherbet. This makes a deliciously refreshing dessert on a hot summer's day.

VEGETABLE JUICE SHERBET
Serves 4

250 ml Skinny
1 x 375 ml can V8 Vegetable Juice
1 teaspoon salt
⅛ teaspoon pepper
2 teaspoons Worcestershire
  sauce

Stir all ingredients together and chill. Either churn or set by the freeze/beat method, cover and ripen for one to two hours in the freezer before serving.

A refreshing way to begin a rich meal on a hot summer's day. Or, as a palate cleanser between courses. A little iced vodka spooned over the sherbet at the time of serving enhances the flavour. Garnish with fresh watercress if available.

APRICOT NECTAR SHERBET
Serves 5

250 ml Skinny
1 x 425 ml can apricot nectar

Mix both ingredients and chill. Either churn or set by the freeze/beat method. Cover. Ripen in the freezer for one to two hours before serving.

Photograph:
Left. Bombe Victoria (see recipe page 62).
Back. Frozen Strawberry Savarin with Raspberry Sauce (see recipe page 55).
Centre. Rocky Road Ice Cream (see recipe page 28).
Cherry Ripe Ice Cream (see recipe page 21).
Chocolate-dipped Ice Cream (see recipe page 77).
Front. Creme de Menthe Ice Cream (see recipe page 55).
Centre right. Smoothy Caramel Mousse (see recipe page 59).

53

GRAND ICED DESSERTS

From easily executed family fare to a spectacular flaming Bombe — a good cross section of iced desserts are represented in this section. There are some old time favourites as well as lots of new ones, which I hope will become favourites.

There are two sponge cakes in this section. They are a chocolate sponge for the Creme de Menthe Ice Cream cake and a plain sponge for the Bombe Alaska. I've used plain flour and cornflour to give a very light result, but you can substitute 1 cup of SR flour in each recipe which replaces the two flours and rising agents, cream of tartar and bicarbonate of soda.

Of course, you can always cheat a little and buy a sponge or make up a packet of sponge cake mix.

ICE CREAM CAKES

There is no reason why you shouldn't leave the liqueur out of the following suggestions. Sprinkle over a little orange juice to keep the sponge cake moist. A layer of finely-chopped glace fruits macerated in liqueur or orange juice would be a lovely filling. Providing that these cakes are kept absolutely airtight in the freezer they will last for up to three weeks and they make excellent birthday cakes (see photograph on page 52). This cake was made in a scalloped form I bought in Italy. You will find a spring form equally useful and attractive.

I've given 5 combinations for ice cream cakes. They should be assembled in the order of the ingredients listed.

PLUM ICE CREAM CAKE

layer of sponge cake, cut to fit the base of a cake pan or ice cream mould
Kirsch, sprinkled over sponge (see page 63)
Plum Ice Cream (see page 16).

garnish:
piped sweetened cream, crystallised rose petals or violets (see page 76), angelica strips.

FIG AND ORANGE ICE CREAM CAKE

Orange Ice Cream (see page 21)
sponge cake, cut to fit cake tin (see page 63)
Kirsch, sprinkled over sponge
Fig Ice Cream, spread over sponge (see page 15)
Chantilly cream (see page 72)
shredded orange rind

STRAWBERRY ICE CREAM

Strawberry Ice Cream (see page 16)
sponge cake, cut to fit over ice cream (see page 63)
orange flavoured liqueur, sprinkled over sponge
Strawberry Ice Cream, repeat first layer
Chantilly cream (see page 72)
frosted whole strawberries (see page 46)

CHOCOLATE ICE CREAM CAKE

Chocolate Ice Cream (see page 25)
sponge cake, cut to fit over Chocolate Ice Cream (see page 63)
Maraschino, sprinkled over sponge
Chantilly cream (see page 72)
Maraschino cherries and toasted hazelnuts, chopped

MOCHA ICE CREAM CAKE

Double Espresso Ice Cream (see page 35)
chocolate sponge cut to fit over ice cream (see page 55)
rum, sprinkled over sponge
Chantilly cream (see page 72)
Chocolate Shapes (see page 77)

NEAPOLITAN ICE CREAMS

Using the base recipe for Neapolitan Ice Cream try making up your own flavours, for example: four ice cream flavours using one cup of each: lemon, vanilla, chocolate and pistachio. Yoghurts too, are successfully frozen in this way as long as you keep in mind the flavours and textures .

NEAPOLITAN ICE CREAM

1 cup Vanilla Ice Cream (see page 15)
1 cup Mocha Ice Cream (see page 39)
1 cup Berry Ice Cream (see page 32)
sponge fingers
Kirsch

Choose a rectangular cake tin which holds one litre (4 cups). It should measure approximately 23 x 10 x 5 cm. Cut sponge fingers (see page 83) to fit the base of the tin. Sprinkle over with liqueur and place in the freezer. Prepare the ice creams, spread one at a time into the tin over the sponge finger base. Freeze each ice cream thoroughly before spreading the next layer on top. When the tin is full cover with foil, tie down securely and leave in the freezer until firm. Dip into warm water, invert over a plate, shake out ice cream. Place serving plate over the top and turn up other way so the sponge fingers are on the base. Return to the freezer, or if very firm leave on the bottom shelf of the refrigerator for up to half an hour before serving. Serve cut into slices.

CHOCOLATE CREAM DE MENTHE ICE CREAM CAKE
Serves 10-12

Chocolate sponge (base):
⅔ cup flour
3 tablespoons cornflour
4 tablespoons cocoa
1 teaspoon cream of tartar
½ teaspoon bicarbonate of soda
4 eggs
½ cup castor sugar
1 tablespoon butter, melted
3 tablespoons hot water
pinch salt
Kahlua, chocolate liqueur (optional)

Prepare a 20 cm spring form tin, generously butter the tin, then flour it and shake out excess flour. Sift dry ingredients. Heat eggs and sugar until thick and creamy. Fold in sifted dry ingredients with butter and water. Pour into tin and bake at 220°C (425°F) for 30-35 minutes or until cooked. Leave the cake in the tin for two minutes, then turn out onto a wire rack to cool.

When cake is cold, sprinkle some sugar over a wooden board and place the cake on this. (The sugar makes the cake easier to turn while you're cutting it.) With a long knife, cut the cake in two. Wash and dry the spring form tin and place half the cake in the bottom. Sprinkle over the, optional, chocolate liqueur, and place in the freezer until the ice cream is ready. Freeze the other half for a future ice cream cake or a chocolate trifle.

CREAM DE MENTHE ICE CREAM

1 litre Smoothy
300 ml thickened cream
2 teaspoons green food colouring
2 teaspoons peppermint essence
1 cup Creme de Menthe

Mix all the ingredients together and chill. Either churn or set by the freeze/beat method. When almost set, spoon over the prepared chocolate base, smooth over the top, cover and freeze overnight.

To serve: Dip the form into warm water, dry the bottom and release the sides. Place on a serving plate with the base still under the cake. Decorate as desired and return to the refrigerator to soften for approx one hour.

This cake can be stored frozen for a week and after decorating can be returned to the freezer for a day. If too hard, leave in the bottom of the refrigerator for half an hour before serving.

FROZEN STRAWBERRY SAVARIN WITH RASPBERRY SAUCE
Serves 8-10

1 kg fresh strawberries
½ cup sugar
6 tablespoons water
300 ml thickened cream
¼ cup Kirsch

Wipe over the strawberries if dirty, but try not to wash them. Hull the strawberries and puree in a food processor or a blender. Failing that, sieve them.

Dissolve the sugar in the water over low heat, stirring all the time until boiling. Take from heat and cool. Whip cream until soft peaks form.

Mix strawberry puree and sugar syrup together, then fold in cream and Kirsch. Leave to mature and chill in the refrigerator for several hours or overnight, then churn or set by the freeze/beat method. When nearly frozen, pour into a wetted 22 cm savarin mould. Cover and freeze until firm. (The mould should hold 1 litre of mixture.) When ready to serve, dip in warm water and invert onto a serving plate. Leave to soften in the bottom of the refrigerator for approximately one hour.

Serve with Raspberry Sauce (see page 72). Fill the centre with fresh flowers, or extra berries, and let guests add their own sauce.

NEAPOLITAN ICE CREAM TRIFLE

Make with 3½ cups ice cream of your choice or 3 different ice creams. For example, a cup of strawberry, a cup of vanilla, and 1½ cups of chocolate. Prepare the trifle the same way as Yoghurt Trifle (see page 92). This is an excellent frozen trifle for preparing ahead for special occasions. It is reasonably quick, inexpensive and very attractive (see photograph 92).

Photograph:
Ice Cream Christmas Pudding (see recipe this page) with Brandy Sauce (see recipe page 71).

ICE CREAM CHRISTMAS PUDDING
Makes 10-12 servings

250 ml Smoothy
600 ml thickened cream
2 eggs, separated
⅓ cup slivered almonds, toasted
⅓ cup red and green glace cherries
⅓ cup mixed chopped peel
⅓ cup raisins
⅓ cup sultanas
⅓ cup currants
1 teaspoon mixed spice
¼ cup rum or sherry
½ teaspoon cinnamon
½ teaspoon nutmeg
⅔ cup icing sugar
2 tablespoons cocoa

Mix all fruits and almonds together and macerate in rum or sherry overnight.

Next day, mix in the spices and cocoa. Beat egg whites stiffly, add yolks beating well, then add half the sugar.

Beat the cream until soft peaks form and add remaining sugar and Smoothy. Fold in the egg white mixture. Pour into a container, cover and freeze until half set. Take from the freezer, beat well and fold in the fruit mixture. Pour into a 2 litre (8 cup) wetted pudding basin, cover with foil and freeze until firm.

When ready to serve, dip the basin into warm water and invert over a serving plate. Leave for one to two hours in the bottom of the refrigerator until the pudding softens a little, but don't let it melt.

Surround with holly and serve, cut into wedges, with brandy sauce.

This pudding may be stored in the freezer for up to three weeks before the festive season and is an excellent dessert for pre-Christmas parties. It is also a welcome change to a traditional pudding on a hot Christmas day.

BRANDY SNAP BASKETS
Makes 8 baskets

2 heaped tablespoons golden syrup
⅓ cup butter
⅓ cup soft brown sugar
½ cup plain flour
2 teaspoons ginger powder
pinch salt

Melt butter with sugar and syrup over a low heat, stirring until all ingredients are combined. Sift ginger, flour and salt and stir into butter mixture.

Drop tablespoonfuls onto greased trays, leaving at least 10 cm around each spoonful for spreading. It is best to plan on cooking four baskets at a time, using two trays. Cook them in a 170°C (340°F) oven, one tray above the other. Cook for ten minutes or until well spread, thin and golden. Leave on trays for one minute, remove carefully with a spatula and immediately make baskets. Using hands, gently mould around the base of a lightly greased milk bottle or jam jar of approximately the same size. Leave for two minutes to harden. Carefully remove from bottle and cool on a wire rack. Store, absolutely airtight. Keep one day.

Note: If brandy snaps harden before you have time to work on them, return to the oven to soften, then proceed.

If you want to make brandy snaps in the traditional shaped 'cigars' make the mixture and drop in teaspoonfuls onto a greased tray leaving about 5 cm spreading space around each one. They will only need five minutes cooking time, one minute resting on the tray after leaving the oven, then wrap around the handle of a woodle spoon.

Fill brandy snap baskets with your favourite ice cream either in scoops or spoonfuls and pass a sauce separately. Any ice cream which goes well with ginger will be a great hit in these little baskets, but my favourite is Morello Cherry Ice Cream.

PINEAPPLE ICE CREAM
Serves 10

1 large ripe pineapple, with top
1 cup pineapple juice
½ cup water
1 cup icing sugar
rind and juice of one orange
300 ml thickened cream
3 tablespoons Maraschino

Place the pineapple on its side and cut one-third off it, lengthwise. Leave whole of green top intact. Keep the remaining third for garnishing.

Using a grapefruit knife or small vegetable knife, carefully remove the flesh from the pineapple skin. Take care not to cut or puncture the skin. Dice the flesh very finely, or chop in a food processor or blender. Do not overwork. It should still have some texture. Mix the pineapple juice, water and sugar together and the finely grated orange rind, in a saucepan. Bring to the boil. Add the pineapple flesh and simmer, uncovered, for 10 minutes. Strain. Reserve the flesh. Return the juices to the pan with orange juice, and reduce over medium heat, uncovered, for a further 15 minutes.

Remove from the heat. Stir in pineapple flesh and cool. Place in the freezer for 1½ to 2 hours, or until beginning to set around the edges. Meanwhile, beat cream to soft peaks and fold in Maraschino. When pineapple mixture is ready, break up with a fork, fold through cream and pile into pineapple shell. Remaining ice cream mixture should be set in a separate container in the freezer. When both mixtures are firm, pile the extra ice cream over the top of the ice cream set in the pineapple shell. Garnish with Chantilly cream and the remaining fresh pineapple, which should be skinned and chopped.

Toasted flaked almonds scattered over the top make a very attractive finish to a refreshing and delicious dessert.

SMOOTHY CARAMEL MOUSSE
Serves 6-8

250 ml Smoothy
6 egg yolks
1 cup sugar
3 tablespoons water
½ cup boiling water, extra
500 ml thickened cream
vanilla flavouring

Dissolve sugar in 3 tablespoons water over low heat stirring until completely dissolved. Bring the mixture to the boil and cook until it forms a brown caramel. Remove from cooker immediately and pour in the boiling water. (Watch your hands — it hisses furiously). Stir and return to a medium heat. Continue to cook until the caramel dissolves, scraping the bottom of the saucepan.

Beat the yolks until light and frothy. Pour in the hot caramel, a little at a time, beating well until the mixture is creamy. Beat in the Smoothy. Set egg yolk mixture over ice, beating while the mixture cools and thickens.

Beat the cream with vanilla until it forms soft peaks, fold into cooled caramel. Pour into a 1¼ litre (5 cup) oblong loaf pan previously rinsed out with cold water, but not dried. Cover and freeze overnight.

To serve: Dip the pan in warm water, invert over a serving plate and shake the mousse out. Garnish with fresh flowers and serve cut into slices.

Remember not to serve the mousse too cold. Rock hard is too cold. It should be of a mousse-like texture, so rest it in the lower part of the refrigerator for approximately one hour before serving.

TULIPE BISCUITS
Makes 12 Tulipes

1 cup flour
1 cup icing sugar
2 x 60 g eggs, plus one extra white

Sift flour and icing sugar together into a medium sized bowl. Using a wooden spoon, beat in the eggs and extra white. Mix well until there are no lumps. Preheat oven to 180°C (350°F). Turn two baking trays, or four Swiss roll tins, upside down. Lightly paint the backs of the tins with melted butter. Make four outlines on the larger trays, using a saucer, or make two outlines on the smaller trays. Using a spatula, spread the mixture evenly and thinly, over the circles outlined. Place in the centre of the oven and cook six minutes exactly. The edges should just be turning golden.

Have teacups or jars ready, turned upside down.

Remove trays from oven. Immediately remove the biscuits, one at a time, with a spatula and place on the bases of the cups or jars. Using your hands, gently mould the Tulipe around the cups. Leave for two minutes, or until set. Place on a cake rack and leave to cool.

Store absolutely airtight until ready to use.

Cook remaining mixture in the same manner to make next batch of Tulipes.

If the biscuits set before they are moulded on the cup bases, return to the oven to soften for approximately one minute. Don't let them cook further.

A clean pair of oven or cotton gloves are a great asset when moulding the hot biscuits.

Tulipes make wonderful bases for ice creams, sherbets, coupes and sundaes. If serving a sauce, it will soften the biscuit, so spoon over at the very last minute before serving or it may be easier to serve sauce separately in a jug.

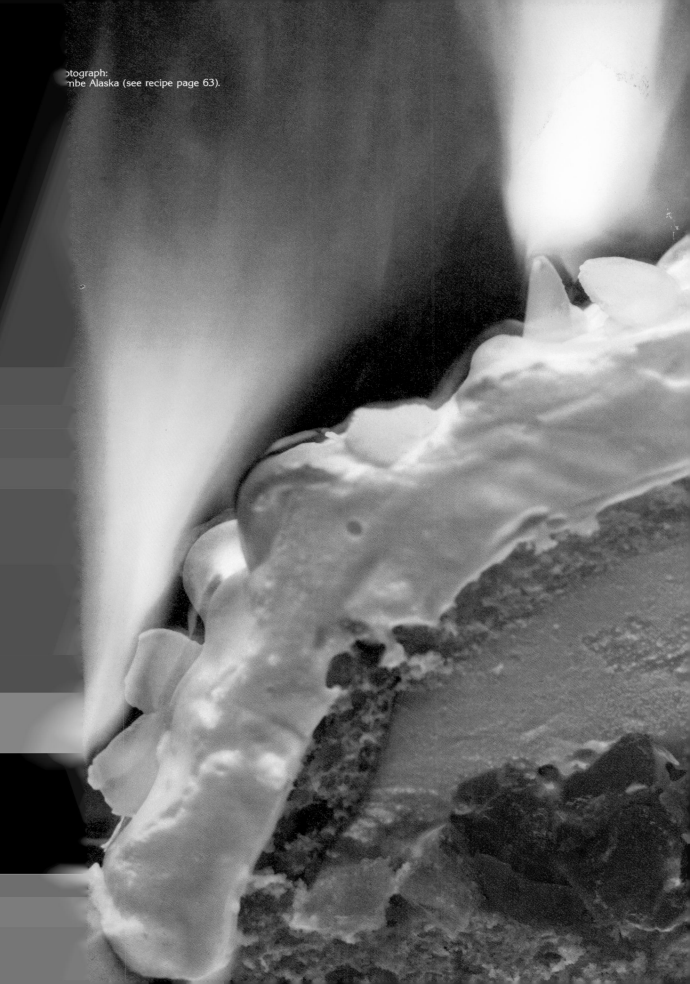

otograph:
mbe Alaska (see recipe page 63).

BOMBES

Bombes are moulded, frozen desserts combining usually two, sometimes three, different types of ices. The best contrasts will be using ice creams from different sections e.g. the custard-based ices with sherbets, or Smoothy ice creams with cream and the rich ice creams.

Choose flavours which compliment each other and keep the textures different. The centre of the bombe can be filled with marinated chopped fruits like glaced fruits, crystallised fruits and so on, or crushed meringues or macaroons sprinkled with a little brandy or liqueur. Garnishes are also important. Try chocolate leaves, curls or shapes. Also crystallised fruits and angelica; and flowers are very pretty. Silver cashews or praline or peanut crackle crushed finely are excellent garnishes. Chantilly cream or liqueur sweetened cream, are very attractive if spooned or piped around the base of the bombe, or you can surround the bombe with fresh fruits or fruit salad.

Creating your own bombes from the many recipes in this book will give you hours of pleasure.

The bombe mould: special bombe moulds are available but any pudding basin or particularly a tall straight-sided jug will serve satisfactorily. Metal and plastic are the best materials to use.

BOMBE VICTORIA
Serves 10

500 ml (2 cups) Vanilla Ice Cream
500 ml (2 cups) Skinny orange sherbet
crystallised violets
Chocolate Leaves

Choose a one litre (4 cup) mould. A tall straight-sided jug is impressive. Place the mould in the freezer to chill.

Make the Vanilla Ice Cream (see page 24). When ice cream is almost set spoon over the base and up the sides of the chilled mould, forming a shell, leaving the centre hollow. If you have any difficulty doing this build up the casing in gradual stages. Cover tightly with foil and tie with string. Place upright in the freezer until very firm approximately one to two hours.

Meanwhile, make the Skinny Orange Sherbet (see page 50). When almost set pile into the centre of the ice cream lined mould. Cover again, chill upright for two hours or until firm.

62

To serve dip mould into warm water, invert on a serving platter, shake ice cream out and immediately return to the freezer to keep firm. Decorate with a base of upstanding Chocolate Leaves (see page 77) or Curls (see page 77). Press the row of Crystallised Violets (see page 76) around the centre and on top of the bombe. Rest in the lower part of the refrigerator for half an hour before serving.

The easiest way to serve a tall mould like this is to cut it in halves across the centre. Lift off the top and cut into wedges then cut the lower half into wedges.

These first two Bombes require a hollow centre to hold the fruits. Prepare second flavouring as for Bombe Victoria and leave to set. Spoon out approximately half a cup of the set mixture (use for cones or a coupe) leaving a 'pocket' for the fruits.

MONT BLANC:
Mocca Ice Cream (see page 39)
Vanilla Ice Cream (see page 24)
glace marrons, chopped finely to fill the centre

BOMBE CARDINAL:
Fresh Peach Ice Cream (see page 16)
Raspberry Sherbet (see page 49)
red currants in syrup, to fill the centre

BOMBE ORIENTALE:
Chocolate Ice Cream (see page 25)
Lemon Sherbet (see page 50)
Chocolate Curls, to surround and pile on top (see page 77)

BOMBE DECEMBER 25TH:
Christmas Mince Ice Cream (see page 20)
Eggnog Ice Cream (see page 19)
Christmas leaves or decorations, to surround

BOMBE SOVEREIGN:
Lemon lemon Ice Cream (see page 31)
Tea Ice Cream (see page 33)
fine slices of lemon, to garnish the outside

BOMBE ALEXANDRA:
Victorian Brown Bread Ice Cream (see page 33)
Morello Cherry Ice Cream (see page 18)
morello cherries chocolate dipped (see page 77), to surround

STRAWBERRY PISTACHIO BOMBE:
Strawberry Ice Cream (see page 16)
Pistachio Ice Cream (see page 27)
fresh whole strawberries and skinned pistachios, scattered over

Bombe Alaska, really is a grand iced dessert. Sometimes called Surprise Omelette (Omelette a la Norvegienne) it has a centre of cold fruits, surrounded with sponge cake and ice cream and a crusty meringue which is browned in a very hot oven. It should be brought flaming to the table with the lights dimmed (page 60), but care must be taken.

To flame alcohol successfully, you should heat approximately 3 tablespoons in a small pan. A Turkish coffee pot, with its long handle is ideal. Hold a lighted match over it, and the alcohol will ignite the moment it reaches the correct temperature. If you over heat it, you burn out the alcohol and it will never light.

A pair of flame proof gloves is a great asset for carrying flaming dishes. Extra warmed alcohol could be lit at the table if you want a great show.

BOMBE ALASKA
Serves 16

1 x 20 cm sponge cake
orange flavoured liqueur
4½ cups Vanilla Ice Cream
90 g flaked almonds, roasted
5 egg whites
¾ cup castor sugar
200 g mixed glace fruits apricots,
    peaches, pineapple, cherries
    chopped and soaked in ¼ cup
    orange juice
warmed brandy to flame

Place the sponge (next recipe) on a cutting board sprinkled with sugar. This makes turning the cake easier for cutting. With a long knife, cut the cake into four layers, turning the cake around the knife. Place two layers side by side on a heat-proof oval platter and trim them to fit within 1 cm of the inner edge, filling up all the gaps with bits of sponge so there is no base of the platter showing. Sprinkle with orange liqueur. Spoon the fruits over the sponge, keeping them 1 cm from the edges. Soften the ice cream (see page 24) a little and spoon over the sponge, moulding higher in the centre and keeping 1 cm from the edge. Smooth over and place in the freezer if beginning to melt. Trim the remaining sponge layers to fit over the top of the ice cream, and fill in all the gaps, so no ice cream shows. Sprinkle with orange liqueur and freeze. The bombe can stay covered with foil like this for up to three weeks. Set the oven rack in the centre of the oven and preheat to 250°C (475°F).

To finish the bombe: Beat the whites with a pinch of salt until firm but still glossy. Beat in the sugar, 2 tablespoons at a time, beating well after each addition. When meringue is firm and glossy, spoon or pipe over prepared bombe, straight from the freezer. Make sure the meringue covers the entire cake, then scatter flaked almonds over meringue.

Rest the platter over an oven-proof dish (like a lasagne dish) filled with ice, and place in the very hot oven for one to two minutes, watching all the time until the meringue is nicely golden. Don't let the ice cream melt, or the meringue burn. Immediately, take to the table, pour the warmed brandy around the bombe and ignite. Serve in slices.

This recipe may be divided to make 2 smaller bombes or one small bombe, in which case it is better to aim for a 20 cm round one. For convenience, it's better to prepare two bases then finish them when the occasion arises. To make a more economical bombe, leave the fruits and almonds out of the recipe.

SPONGE BASE FOR BOMBE ALASKA
I find this a very easy sponge to make and you won't find a better one for feather lightness. Because it rises so well, it is easy to cut into four layers, as required for the large Bombe Alaska.

⅔ cup cornflour
2 tablespoons flour
1 teaspoon cream of tartar
½ teaspoon bicarbonate of soda
½ cup castor sugar
4 eggs (60 g eggs)
pinch salt

Separate whites and yolks of eggs. Beat whites and salt until stiff. Add sugar gradually, beating until stiff, then add the yolks one at a time. Beat until thick and creamy. Fold in sifted flours and rising agents. Pour into two butter-brushed and floured 20 cm sandwich pans and bake in the centre of a pre-heated oven at 200°C (400°F) for about 25 minutes or until receding from the sides of the pans, and golden on top. Leave in the pans for one minute before turning out onto a wire rack.

These sponges freeze for up to three months, if stored in an airtight plastic bag.

ICE CREAM PROFITEROLES
Serves 8-10

Profiteroles:
1 cup milk
pinch salt
1 teaspoon castor sugar
100 g butter
1 cup flour
3 x 60 g eggs

filling:
2-3 cups softened ice cream
sauce:
hot chocolate

To make profiteroles heat milk, salt, sugar and butter in medium size saucepan and bring to the boil. Immediately it boils pour in all the flour and stir constantly with a wooden spoon off the cooker. When it is lump free return to a medium heat stirring all the time to evaporate any excess moisture. Turn out onto a dinner plate to cool. Pre-heat oven to 220°C (425°F) and set the rack in the centre

oven. Beat in the eggs one by one beating well after each addition until all eggs have been incorporated. The mixture should be very shiny and smooth. Fit a large piping bag with a 1½ cm star tube. Pipe approximately 20 profiteroles onto a lightly greased baking tray leaving room for expansion.

Bake 15-20 minutes until golden. Reduce the temperature to 200°C (400°F) and prop open the oven door with the handle of a wooden spoon. Cook a further 15-20 minutes. When profiteroles are crisp, remove from oven and cut a small slit in the base of each (this is to let out the steam). Leave to cool on a wire rack. If storing they must be kept absolutely air-tight or they will go soft. They keep three days in the refrigerator.

To fill profiteroles, soften ice cream to a good piping consistency. Spoon into a piping bag fitted with a 1½ cm plain tube. Cut a suitable

Photograph:
Ice Cream Profiteroles (see recipe this page).

hole in the base of each profiterole and force in as much ice cream as each will hold. Place on a baking sheet. Set in the freezer until firm.

Pile the profiteroles in a pyramid in a pretty glass serving dish. Heat Chocolate Sauce (see page 75) and spoon a little over the tops of the profiteroles. Serve the remaining sauce in a jug at the table. There are many ice creams suitable for this recipe. Those which I love with chocolate sauce are honey, pear and ginger, coffee, orange, mocha, raspberry, pistachio and strawberry.

SOUTH PACIFIC PIE
Serves 8-10

Crust:
1½ cups desiccated coconut
¼ cup castor sugar
60 g butter, melted
filling:
2 cups Banana Ice Cream
1 x 425 g can crushed pineapple,
    drained
garnish:
red glaced cherries
Chocolate Curls

To make the crust mix all ingredients together and pat into 24 cm pie plate. Cook in the centre of a pre-heated oven at 150°C (300°F) for 15-20 minutes or until coconut crust is golden. Remove from oven and leave to cool. Make Banana Ice Cream (see page 41). Spread nearly set ice cream into cooled crust, smooth over the top with a spatula and freeze until firm. Drain crushed pineapple, spread over ice cream and decorate with cherries and Chocolate Curls (see page 77). Serve at once.

Any of the following ice cream flavours could be substituted for banana. ginger, chocolate, orange, paw paw or mango.

ICE CREAM CHOCOLATE ROLL
Serves 8-10

Chocolate Roll:
6 x 60 g eggs, separated
¾ cup castor sugar
200 g cooking chocolate, chopped
    roughly
4 tablespoons water
Filling:
½ litre (2 cups) ice cream, vanilla,
    ginger, mocca, strawberry or other
    favourite flavour, which goes well
    with chocolate

Line a Swiss roll tin measuring 25 x 30 cm approximately, with greaseproof paper. Brush over paper with melted butter. Pre-heat oven to 200°C (400°F).

Melt chocolate and water together over a water bath on low heat stirring from time to time with a wooden spoon. Beat yolks and sugar together until pale and light. Beat whites in another bowl until they are glossy and hold stiff peaks. Cool chocolate mixture slightly and beat into egg yolk mixture. Fold in whites using a rubber spatula. Spoon batter into prepared tin and bake in the centre oven for 25 minutes. Don't open the oven during cooking until the roll is risen, firm on top and receding from the sides of the tin. It may be necessary to place paper over the roll for the last five minutes or so of cooking to prevent browning.
Remove from oven in a draught-free atmosphere. Leave in the tin two minutes. Turn out onto a clean tea-towel. Working from the short end of the roll, roll up firmly, but with light hands. Don't squash it! Use the towel to assist you to roll. Leave like this on a cake rack to cool.

Meanwhile prepare ice cream according to your favourite recipe. When almost set it is ready to spread over the cooled roll. Unroll the chocolate roll and spread with softened ice cream. Roll up again, trim the ends and place on a serving dish. Cover and return to the freezer until half an hour before serving. If the roll is too firm place in the bottom of the refrigerator for up to half an hour before serving. Cut into slices and serve with fresh flowers to decorate, or sliced fresh fruits to eat! Mandarine segments are delicious.

Serve a suitable sauce to accompany this roll if you wish.

ICE CREAM FILLED PAVLOVA
Serves 8

Pavlova:
3 egg whites
pinch of salt
1 cup castor sugar
1 tablespoon cornflour
1 teaspoon lemon juice

filling:
2-3 cups ice cream, of your choice
diced fruits
sauce, (optional)

To make pavlova:
Beat egg whites with salt until firm and
glossy. Beat in ¾ of the castor sugar 1
tablespoon at a time beating well after each
addition. Continue to beat until sugar
dissolves. Mix cornflour with remaining
sugar and fold into meringue with lemon
juice. Lightly butter an oven tray and mark a
23 cm ring in the centre by drawing with a
finger in the butter around the cake tin. Pile
meringue into a piping bag fitted with a large
star tube. Pipe a circle first following the line
then fill in and finally build the sides leaving a
good hollow centre for ice cream filling.
Bake in the centre of a pre-heated oven
100°C (200°F) for 1¼-1½ hours or until
pavlova is dry. Cool in the oven. Store
air-tight until ready for filling and serving.

To serve, place pavlova on a large serving
plate. Pile ice cream scooped or spooned
into the centre. Scatter over with diced fruits
or any garnish which is suitable. Pass a
complimentary sauce separately.

Here are two ideas for filling pavlovas with ice
cream:

PEPPERMINT CRISP PAVLOVA

Peppermint Crisp Ice Cream (see page 43)
Chocolate Sauce (see page 75)
extra peppermint crisp, crushed.

Individual pavlova cases:
The pavlova mixture in the recipe for Ice
Cream Filled Pavlova (see page 67) will
make three to four individual bases
measuring approximately 8 cm each
depending on how adept you are at forming
pavlova cases. Bake for 1-1¼ hours and fill
as in the main recipe.

TROPICAL PAVLOVA

Mango Ice Cream (see page 41)
diced pineapple or sliced bananas dipped in
lemon juice
Orange Sauce (see page 72), served
separately

ICE CREAM PIE
Serves 8

Crust:
1 x 225 g packet ginger nut biscuits
90 g melted butter
filling:
1 x 425 g can pie apples
2 cups Lemon Ice Cream
garnish:
150 ml thickened cream
lemon rind, finely grated
castor sugar, to taste
dark chocolate, grated

Work biscuits to fine crumbs in a food
processor or blender or crush in a heavy duty
plastic bag with a heavy object. Mix in melted
butter and spread into base of a 24 cm pie
plate or springform and refrigerate for 1
hour. Prepare ice cream (see page 17).

Spoon pie apples into crust. Spread nearly
set lemon ice cream over apples and smooth
over with a spatula. Freeze for approximately
one hour or until firm.

Beat cream with enough sugar to sweeten
and fold in lemon rind. Pipe rosettes around
outer edge of pie, grate chocolate over the
cream and either freeze or serve at once.

If making in advance this pie must be stored
in the deep freeze. When the cream is set
hard, cover with plastic and leave frozen until
needed. To defrost leave on the bottom shelf
of the refrigerator for approximately one
hour in summer and two hours in winter so
that the Lemon Ice Cream has a firm but
mousse-like consistency.

An excellent recipe for making up in
quantities for big parties and buffets. It will
store well, frozen for up to three weeks. Don't
refreeze once it has thawed.

The lemon ice cream could be changed for
any one of the following recipes: orange ice
cream, rhubarb, honey, passionfruit, vanilla
or chocolate, or any flavour which goes well
with apples.

ICED APRICOT SOUFFLE
Serves 10

500 ml Smoothy
1½ cups sugar
200 g dried apricots
3 tablespoons lemon juice
½ cup water
150 ml thickened cream
4 egg whites
few grains salt

garnish:
150 ml thickened cream
5 glace apricots
apricot brandy
angelica

Soak apricots in water and lemon juice for half an hour. Add sugar and simmer gently for several minutes or until fruit softens. Prepare an 18 or 20 cm souffle dish with a collar. Fold a double strip of foil 15 cm wide to go around the top of the souffle dish and overlap by at least 8 cm. The foil should stand a good 10 cm above the rim of the dish. Stick down with tape; one which will not come unstuck in a humid atmosphere.

Puree apricots in a food processor or blender or chop very finely. Stir in Smoothy and leave to cool. Beat cream until it forms soft peaks and fold into apricot mixture.

Beat egg whites with salt until firm and glossy. Fold into apricot mixture. Pour into prepared souffle dish and place level in the freezer until firm, preferably overnight.

To serve: remove collar. Beat cream with apricot brandy to taste, until firm. Pile into a piping bag fitted with a large star tube. Pipe ten swirls of cream on top of the souffle. Slit glace apricots in halves and place in each swirl of cream. Make angelica leaves placing decoratively around apricot halves. Return to freezer until ready to serve. If too firm place in the lower part of the refrigerator for approximately half an hour before serving. It is important that this dessert be served at a mousse-like consistency.

Photographed:
Iced Apricot Souffle (see recipe this page).

ICED PLUM SOUFFLE
Serves 10

500 ml Smoothy
2 cups plum puree
150 ml thickened cream
4 egg whites
few grains salt

garnish:
150 ml thickened cream
Maraschino
10 whole skinned hazelnuts, toasted

Make plum puree as in Plum Ice Cream (see page 16). Prepare plum souffle the same way as in Iced Apricot Souffle, (see page 69) and garnish.

ICED FIG SOUFFLE
Serves 10

500 ml Smoothy
2 cups fig puree
150 ml thickened cream
4 egg whites
few grains salt

garnish:
150 ml thickened cream
orange-flavoured liqueur
Chocolate Curls

Prepare fig puree as in Fig Ice Cream (see page 15). Finish recipe according to Iced Apricot Souffle, (see page 69).

ICED PISTACHIO SOUFFLE
Serves 6

¾ cup peeled pistachios, chopped
¾ cup castor sugar
3 eggs separated
300 ml thickened cream
1 tablespoon Kirsch
praline powder

Prepare a 2½ cup souffle dish with a collar, (see Iced Apricot Souffle, page 69). Beat egg yolks and sugar until very pale and the mixture "ribbons". It's quicker to do this over hot water. Fold in pistachios and Kirsch. Beat cream until it forms soft peaks and fold into mixture. Beat egg whites until firm and fold into pistachio mixture. Spoon into prepared mould and leave to set in the deep freeze. Remove collar when firm and garnish with praline (see page 78) scattered over the top.

FROZEN BERRY SOUFFLE
Serves 6

250 g berries, fresh or frozen
½ cup castor sugar or to taste
1 cup thickened cream
Kirsch
4 egg whites

Prepare a 2½ cup souffle dish with collar, see Iced Apricot Souffle, as in the other recipes. Puree berries with sugar. Whip cream until it forms soft peaks. Beat egg whites until stiff and glossy. Fold cream into berry mixture with Kirsch to taste. Lastly, fold in egg whites. Turn into prepared souffle dish set level in the deep freeze until firm. Garnish with extra berries scattered over the top.

Berries can be any of the following: strawberries, raspberries, loganberries, youngberries, blackberries or boysenberries.

MELON A LA CHARTREUSE
Serves 1 per person

½ small cantaloup melon
1 tablespoon green or yellow
   Chartreuse
scoops of Vanilla Ice Cream

Scrape the seeds out of the melon. Pour in Chartreuse and chill until serving time. Spoon in scoops of ice cream (see page 24) and serve immediately.

PROBLEMS SOLVED

CRYSTALLISED ICE CREAM:

The Causes:

1 Mixture is too lean, ie., too low in fats. Add more cream and/or enrich with egg yolks which don't necessarily need cooking.

2 Mixture too acid. Highly acidic fruits like citrus and pineapple are more suitable with a rich base.

3 Too high in enzymes. Fruits like pineapple, pawpaw and Kiwi fruits contain an enzyme which breaks down the protein in milk or cream, so the fruits must be cooked to inactivate the enzyme. Or, opt for the easy way out and use canned or bottled fruits (see base recipe page 24).

4 Churned the mixture too fast. This can only happen with hand churning. The motorized models are geared to the correct speed.

5 Too much salt mixed with the ice. It lowers the temperature, and freezing takes place too quickly.

SAUCES AND TOPPINGS

Many of these sauces can be served hot or cold. Most can be made in advance, and they store well in the refrigerator.

Thick sauces will often set when left to cool, all that is necessary is to reheat over hot water or a very low heat. If too thick, thin with a little water.

One cup of sauce is enough for approximately ¾ litre (3 cups) ice cream or 6 servings.

The crowning glory: chocolate curls and shapes and other exciting ideas for dressing up your ice cream creations.

Or try Chocolate-Dipped Ice Cream: A superb, quick-setting coating for frozen ice cream. Ice creams firmly wedged into cones can be dipped, or scoops of your favourite ice creams. Ginger, banana, raspberry, strawberrry, coffee, pear, vanilla, cherry ripe, coconut ice, pineapple, pistachio, melon, Creme de Menthe, peppermint crisp and many other flavours are complimented by chocolate. Try other flavours chocolate-dipped. You will be surprised at your success — it's so easy.

BRANDY SAUCE
Makes 1⅔ cups

300 ml water
3 cloves
⅓ cup dark brown sugar
rind of 1 lemon
rind of half an orange
1 bay leaf
½ teaspoon cinnamon
½ teaspoon mixed spice
2½ teaspoons cornflour
2 tablespoons brandy

Pare rinds from citrus fruits using a vegetable peeler, taking care not to remove any of the white pith. (Pith will make the sauce bitter.) Cook rinds in water with sugar, spices and bay leaf for 10 minutes. Blend cornflour into brandy and stir into sauce until it thickens. Cook a further two minutes then strain off bay leaf, rinds and cloves. Cool with a circle of greaseproof paper directly on top of the sauce to prevent a skin from forming. Serve at room temperature with Ice Cream Christmas Pudding (see page 57).

The addition of ½ cup of currants, sultanas or raisins cooked in this sauce gives it texture and makes approximately 2½ cups.

RAISIN SAUCE
Makes 1½ cups

⅔ cup raisins
1¼ cups water
½ teaspoon cinnamon
½ teaspoon mixed spice
pinch ground cloves
⅓ cup dark brown sugar
rind of 1 lemon
rind of half an orange
2 teaspoons cornflour
3 tablespoons Drops on the Rocks (Whisky base liqueur), brandy or sherry

Plump raisins in Drops on the Rocks for half an hour. Pare rinds from citrus fruits with a vegetable peeler, taking just the rind, no pith. (White pith will make the sauce bitter.) Using a very sharp knife, cut the strips of rind into fine julienne (matchsticks). Cook raisins in the water with cinnamon, mixed spice, cloves and sugar for 10 minutes. Drop in the citrus rinds. Mix cornflour with 1 tablespoon of water and stir into sauce. Cook, stirring until the sauce thickens and coats the back of a wooden spoon.

To prevent skin from forming on the sauce, place a circle of greaseproof paper directly on the top of the sauce until ready to serve.

PASSIONFRUIT SAUCE
Makes 1⅓ cups

6 passionfruit
1 cup water
2 teaspoons sugar, or to taste
2 teaspoons cornflour

Halve passionfruit and scrape out pulp with a teaspoon. Mix cornflour with a little of the water. Place the rest of the water with the pulp and the sugar in a small saucepan. Stir with a wooden spoon until mixture is boiling. Stir in cornflour and cook for three minutes on reduced heat stirring all the time, until the sauce is thick. Serve hot or cold.

Passionfruit sauce is superb with many ice creams, especially honey ice cream (see page 28).

ORANGE SAUCE
Makes 1½ cups

2 oranges
½ cup water
½ cup castor sugar
¼ cup orange juice concentrate
1 tablespoon orange-flavoured
 liqueur
2 tablespoons cornflour

In a small saucepan bring the water and sugar to simmer, stirring all the time, until the sugar dissolves. With a vegetable peeler, pare the rind off one orange taking just the rind and none of the white pith. With a very sharp knife, cut the strips of rind into fine julienne (matchsticks). Drop the rinds into the simmering sugar syrup and continue to cook gently for a further eight minutes. Mix cornflour and liqueur together. Peel both oranges with a very sharp knife, removing rind and pith. Cut over a plate into segments catching the juice from the oranges. Remove syrup from heat, stir in cornflour mixture. Return to heat to thicken, stirring with a wooden spoon. Cook a further two minutes. Remove from heat. Stir in orange concentrate, orange segments and juices. Cool and serve chilled over ice cream.

Very good with vanilla, chocolate, rhubarb, raspberry, Kiwi Fruit, and many other ices, frozen yoghurts and sherbets.

APRICOT ALMOND SAUCE
Makes 1⅛ cups

1 cup apricot conserve
2 tablespoons slivered almonds,
 toasted
2 teaspoons rum

Heat apricot conserve gently in a small pan until beginning to bubble. Stir in rum. Mix with a wooden spoon and remove from the heat. Stir in almonds and serve hot or cold.

Store in the refrigerator for up to one month.

CHANTILLY CREAM
Makes 1¼ cups

300 ml thickened cream, chilled
¼ cup vanilla sugar

Beat cream and sugar together until the cream forms soft peaks.

This simple vanilla flavoured cream is one of the bases for many ice cream coupes, sundaes and classic ice cream dishes. Instead of vanilla sugar the same amount of castor sugar can be used with a dash of vanilla.

BRANDIED FRUITS
Makes 2 litres

1 x 450 g can pineapple pieces
1 x 425 g can sliced yellow peaches
1 x 425 g can pitted black cherries
½ cup sultanas
½ cup raisins
½ cup prunes, stoned and
 chopped into large pieces
½ cup slivered almonds
½ cup hazelnuts, skinned
¾ cup sugar
1½ cups brandy

Drain the syrup from the pineapple and peaches into a large saucepan. Add sultanas, raisins, prunes and sugar and simmer uncovered, stirring from time to time, until the juices are reduced by approximately ⅓ of the original volume and a syrupy consistency is reached. This will take approximately 30 minutes. Cool. Then add all remaining ingredients. Spoon into two l litre jars and refrigerate. Keeps approximately one month.

Bottled into smaller jars, this recipe makes a wonderful present.

COLD RASPBERRY OR STRAWBERRY SAUCE
Makes 1¼ cups

250 g raspberries or strawberries,
 fresh or frozen
⅓-½ cup castor sugar, or to taste
1-2 tablespoons Kirsch

Puree the berries with the sugar and Kirsch, then pass through a sieve. Pour into a sauce jug and chill before serving.

HOT STRAWBERRY SAUCE
Makes 1 cup

4 tablespoons strawberry jam
½ cup water
1 tablespoon cornflour
1 tablespoon sugar
lemon juice to taste
red food colouring

Mix cornflour with 1 tablespoon of the water. Combine jam, remaining water and sugar in a small saucepan and heat until bubbling. Stir in cornflour and cook for two minutes, stirring all the time with a wooden spoon. Add lemon juice to taste and enrich the colour with a little red colouring.
Serve hot.

JAM SAUCE
Makes 1 cup

4 tablespoons jam of your choice
1 cup water
1 tablespoon cornflour
1 tablespoon sugar
lemon juice to taste
food colouring (same as colour of jam)

Make the sauce exactly the same way as the Hot Strawberry Sauce (see page 73). Add food colouring to give jam a stronger colour.

This sauce may be made with your favourite jam, or any jam you may have in your pantry. Serve hot or cold.

ORANGE LEMON SAUCE
Makes 1⅔ cups

½ cup sugar
1 tablespoon cornflour
1 cup water
2 tablespoons butter
3 tablespoons lemon juice
grated rind of 1 orange and 1 lemon

Mix the cornflour and sugar with water. Stirring constantly, cook over low heat until the sauce is clear and thickened. Stir in butter, juice and grated rinds and cook 1 minute. Leave to cool with a circle of greaseproof paper directly on top of sauce to prevent a skin from forming.

MELBA SAUCE
Makes ¾ cup

200 g raspberries
icing sugar, to taste
lemon juice, to taste

Sieve raspberries, sweeten with a little sieved icing sugar if necessary, and a drop or two of lemon juice.

MARBLED CHOCOLATE MARSHMALLOW SAUCE
Makes 2½ cups

200 g cooking chocolate
1 cup icing sugar, sieved
1 cup Smoothy
8 white marshmallows
vanilla flavouring

Snip each marshmallow into four with a pair of scissors. Place chocolate, icing sugar, vanilla and half a cup of Smoothy into a small saucepan and heat gently. In another small saucepan, heat the snipped marshmallows with the other half cup of Smoothy. When both mixtures are thoroughly melted and smooth, pour the chocolate mixture into a serving bowl and gently swirl the marshmallow in using a fork. Do not mix too much — leave it marbled.

CHOCOLATE MARSHMALLOW SAUCE
Makes 2½ cups

200 g cooking chocolate
1 cup icing sugar, sieved
1 cup Smoothy
8 white marshmallows
vanilla flavouring

Snip each marshmallow into four with a pair of scissors. Place all ingredients into small saucepan. Heat gently, stirring from time to time, until chocolate and marshmallows melt.

Serve hot or warm. If left to get cold, this sauce will set. May be covered and stored in the refrigerator for up to four weeks.

For future servings: Heat gently over warm water before serving.

WALNUT SAUCE
Makes 2 cups

2 cups soft brown sugar
2 tablespoons Smoothy
pinch salt
½ cup thickened cream
½ cup walnut pieces, finely
   chopped

Slowly heat sugar and Smoothy with salt and stir, all the time, until sugar dissolves. Add cream and walnuts and cook until combined.

MORELLO CHERRY SAUCE
Makes 2-2½ cups

(approx. 400 g) jar pitted Morello
   Cherries
pinch cinnamon
¼ cup dry red wine
1 orange
1 tablespoon red currant jelly
2 teaspoons cornflour
2 teaspoons cherry brandy

Drain syrup off cherries and discard. Put cherries in a saucepan with the cinnamon and wine, bring to a simmer and cook, uncovered, for 10 minutes. Grate the orange rind on a coarse grater and then squeeze the juice from the orange. Add rind, juice and jelly to the sauce. Simmer gently until jelly melts and combines with the other ingredients. Remove from the heat. Mix cornflour with 1 tablespoon of water and stir into the mixture. Return to the cooker and thicken, stirring all the time. When the sauce is thick, pour in the cherry brandy.

Serve hot or cold over ice cream.

HOT MOCHA SAUCE
Makes 3 cups

125 g cooking chocolate
1 tablespoon instant coffee powder
2 tablespoons butter
2 tablespoons pure icing sugar
1 cup thickened cream

Break chocolate into small pieces and slowly melt with coffee powder, butter and sugar over water bath stirring with a wooden spoon. Fold in cream and heat until combined.

MARSHMALLOW TOPPING
Makes ¾ cup

1 cup marshmallows
2 tablespoons water
vanilla flavouring

Cut the marshmallows into four pieces with scissors. Dissolve with the water in a small saucepan over a water bath. Simmer gently stirring with a wooden spoon until melted. Stir in vanilla. Serve immediately while still hot.

This topping will set if left to get cold but can be reheated over hot water.

A delicious, light, frothy topping for ice creams and milk drinks.

WHIPPED CHOCOLATE CREAM
Makes 2½ cups

1 cup Smoothy
200 g cooking chocolate
2 tablespoons Kahlua (chocolate
   liqueur)
½ cup thickened cream

Break chocolate into small pieces. Gently heat chocolate and Smoothy over a water bath, until melted. Stir in liqueur and cool. Beat cream and fold into chocolate mixture. Leave with a pretty marbled effect.

CARAMEL MARSHMALLOW SAUCE
Makes 1⅔ cups

Caramel Sauce
6 white marshmallows

Snip marshmallows into fours, using a pair of scissors. Add to Caramel Sauce (see page 75) ingredients. Stir with a wooden spoon. When sauce is smooth and marshmallows have melted, the sauce is ready to serve.

Serve while still warm to hot. If left to get too cold it will be very thick.

MARMALADE SAUCE
Makes 1 cup

½ cup fine textured orange
   marmalade
½ cup apricot jam
2 tablespoons Maraschino

Heat orange marmalade and jam together in a small saucepan. Stir until well combined. Stir in Maraschino and serve.

DARK CHOCOLATE SAUCE
Makes 2 cups

100 g cooking chocolate
1½ tablespoons butter
1½ tablespoons icing sugar
¾ cup thickened cream

Break chocolate into small pieces and slowly melt with butter and sugar over a water bath stirring with a wooden spoon. Add cream and heat until thoroughly mixed. Cool and serve with ice creams.

An excellent sauce with fruits, especially pears.

PINEAPPLE GINGER MARSHMALLOW SAUCE
Makes 1 cup

1 cup crushed pineapple with syrup
1 tablespoon ginger marmalade
1 tablespoon cornflour
1 tablespoon water
10 pink marshmallows

Snip the marshmallows into quarters using scissors. Heat pineapple and syrup with marmalade in a small saucepan. Mix cornflour and water together, add to pineapple mixture and cook for three minutes, stirring all the time. When the sauce is thick and clear, stir in the marshmallows. Heat gently without stirring until marshmallows melt. Pour into a serving dish and gently swirl marshmallows around in the dish, using a fork.

This attractive sauce is delicious, served hot or cold, over vanilla ice cream.

GINGER SAUCE
Makes 1 cup

1 cup ginger marmalade
1 tablespoon cornflour
1 cup water
lemon juice to taste

Mix cornflour with 1 tablespoon of the water. Heat marmalade with remaining water in a small saucepan until simmering. Stir in cornflour and cook for three minutes, stirring all the time. Add lemon juice and serve hot or cold.

CARAMEL SAUCE
Makes 1⅔ cups

½ cup golden syrup
½ cup soft brown sugar
125 g butter
½ cup thickened cream
vanilla flavouring

Cut butter into small pieces. Melt in a saucepan with all other ingredients over a water bath, stirring from time to time. When completely combined, simmer for two minutes. Cool, bottle and store in the refrigerator.

Serve hot or cold.

CHOCOLATE LIQUEUR SAUCE
Makes ¾ cup

125 g cooking chocolate
¼ cup Smoothy
1 tablespoon Tia Maria or Creme De Cacao

Break chocolate into small pieces. Add Smoothy and melt gently over water bath. When melted, stir in liqueur and serve.

Delicious with apricot, peach, berry, and paw paw ice creams.

HOT FUDGE SAUCE
Makes 3 cups

125 g cooking chocolate
2 tablespoons butter
2 tablespoons pure icing sugar
1 cup thickened cream
2 teaspoons brandy

Break chocolate into small pieces and slowly melt with butter and sugar over a water bath, stirring with a wooden spoon. Add cream and brandy and heat until well combined. Serve hot, over very cold ice cream.

Also delicious cool. Left to chill the sauce will set. It may be reheated again over a water bath for future use.

Stores well in the refrigerator.

LEMON SAUCE
Makes 1½ cups

1 lemon
1½ tablespoons golden syrup
1 teaspoon butter
300 ml water
1½ tablespoons sugar
1 tablespoon cornflour

Using a vegetable peeler, pare the rind off the lemon. Cut into fine julienne (matchsticks) using a very sharp knife. Squeeze the juice from the lemon. Mix cornflour with 1 tablespoon of the water. In a small saucepan, heat golden syrup, butter, sugar and remaining water and rinds. When gently boiling, stir in the cornflour and cook for three minutes, stirring all the time with a wooden spoon. When thickened, remove from the fire and stir in lemon juice.

Leave to cool. Store in the refrigerator.

MOCK MAPLE SYRUP
Makes 1 cup

4 tablespoons golden syrup
⅓ cup water
7 tablespoons honey
1 tablespoon lemon juice

Mix all ingredients together in a small saucepan. Heat gently until boiling, stirring from time to time with a wooden spoon. Boil slowly, uncovered, for five minutes or so, until reduced to approximately one cup.

PEANUT CRACKLE

125 g salted peanuts, roasted and skinned
2 cups sugar

Cover the bottom of a lightly-greased swiss roll tin with peanuts. Put the sugar into a heavy-based frying pan, and stir over medium heat until it has melted and is a light brown colour. Be very careful not to let it burn. Pour at once over the peanuts and stand until hard.

Place in a heavy plastic bag and crush with a meat mallet or other heavy object. Store in an airtight container.

Use to top fruit ice cream. Particularly good over peach ice cream.

CRYSTALLISED VIOLETS

fresh violets
egg white
pure icing sugar, sifted

Trim violet stems so that there is just enough to hold on to (about 2 cm). Using a fork, break up an egg white to soften it — don't beat air bubbles into it. Very lightly oil a baking tray, lined with foil. Use a vegetable oil. (Do not use olive oil — it will flavour the violets.) Dip violets, one at a time, into the egg white, shaking off the excess, then into icing sugar, again shaking off excess. Place face up on the prepared tray. Leave in a warm place to dry for approximately eight hours. Lift off with a spatula carefully easing the violets away from the foil. Store in a dark place in air tight glass jars. Crystallised flowers lose their colour when exposed to the light.

Note: Blooms freshly picked in the sun will give a lovely musk flavour. Rose petals may be treated in the same manner.

Stored properly, these will keep up to three weeks and are excellent for garnishing ice creams, cakes and tarts or pies.

LEMON CRUNCH
Makes ¾ cup

1 teaspoon lemon rind, finely grated
2 tablespoons melted butter
3 tablespoons sugar
½ cup crushed cornflakes

Mix all ingredients together. Spread or sprinkle over the top of your favourite ice cream.

CHOCOLATE DIPPING MIXTURE

100 g cooking chocolate
80 ml (4 tablespoons) poly-
    unsaturated vegetable oil

Break chocolate into small pieces. Melt with oil over hot water stirring with a wooden spoon from time to time. When thoroughly melted, the mixture is ready for dipping.

Stores well in the refrigerator. For future use; reheat and melt thoroughly. Once again, mixture is ready for dipping.

Tips for making chocolate dipping easy: Ice cream must be very firm. Don't use a soft ice cream, like a pure cream or custard-based ice. Smoothy ices are best for this.

CHOCOLATE CURLS

cooking chocolate

Break chocolate into small pieces and melt gently over a water bath. Stir with a wooden spoon and when completey melted, spread evenly on the back of a baking tray with a spatula. It's important that there are no sides to the tray, which is why I suggest a baking tray back. When chocolate clouds over it is beginning to set. Wait a few minutes more and before it sets solid, make chocolate curls by scraping the top surface with a spatula.

To make uniform curls: Mark the chocolate into strips the width you have chosen for the curls. Take hold of the spatula, gripping the blade at both ends with your fingers. Drag across the top of the chocolate towards you. The chocolate should roll around itself as you move the spatula.

The thickness of the curl depends on the pressure exerted on the spatula, so that the harder you press, the thicker the curl will be.

To make "free-form" curls: Using the entire surface of the chocolate, scrape the spatula across the surface towards you, picking up large and small curls as you work.

Use for garnishing cakes, ice cream, and pies.

To store, place in single layers in air tight boxes in the freezer.

CHOCOLATE SHAPES

100 g cooking chocolate
20 g Copha

Break chocolate into small pieces and cut Copha approximately the same size. Melt together over water bath, stirring from time to time with a wooden spoon until thoroughly combined. Cover an oven tray with foil.

To make "free-form" chocolate discs: Drop a teaspoon of mixture at a time on to the foil. Using the back of a spoon, spread into a round shape. Leave to set. (In summer set in the refrigerator.) Lift off the foil with a spatula and use for garnishing.

To make chocolate squares and other fancy shapes: Spread melted chocolate mixture evenly over a foil-covered baking tray. Leave until almost set, but not hard. Cut into shapes, using a ruler to mark squares, and biscuit or petits fours cutters to mark shapes. Leave to cool. When cold, lift shapes out with a spatula and use for garnishing. Excess chocolate mixture may be melted down again for future use.

Chocolate decorations must be stored in the refrigerator, preferably in air-tight containers.

Note: On hot days keep chocolate decorations chilled until the very last moment. A good way to handle them is with wooden tongs or chilled metal ones.

This mixture is also excellent for dipping biscuits into. (Like sponge fingers). It gives a very good coating.

CHOCOLATE LEAVES

cooking chocolate
fresh camelia, rose or ivy leaves

Break chocolate into small pieces and melt slowly over a water bath. Stir with a wooden spoon to ensure there are no lumps in the chocolate. Wipe over the surface of leaves with a damp cloth and dry thoroughly. Cover a baking tray with foil. Spread melted chocolate over the top surface of the leaves and place them, chocolate side up, on the foil to dry. In hot weather, it may be necessary to set the leaves in the refrigerator. When chocolate is set, very carefully pull the leaf away from the chocolate. Obviously, it is better to bend the leaf rather than the chocolate which would break. Store chocolate leaves in a cool place until ready to use.

CHOCOLATE BRANDIED CHERRIES

whole cherries with stalks
brandy
Chocolate Dipping Mixture

Pack cherries in a glass jar. Top up with brandy. Fit lid and store for three months before using.

Drain as many cherries as needed and chill for half an hour in the freezer. Meanwhile, prepare Chocolate Dipping Mixture (see page 77). Cover an oven tray with foil. Dip very cold cherries into chocolate mixture letting excess chocolate run off. Stand upright on foil and leave to harden. Use to garnish ice creams and cakes.

Note: These do not store well after dipping, therefore only make as many as you need. Brandied cherries will store for many months.

The best jars to use are Mason's, which have a clamp-on lid with a rubber seal. Otherwise use screw-top jars with plastic lids. Metal lids can taint the fruit.

PRALINE POWDER
Makes ¾ cup

¼ cup blanched almonds, hazelnuts
  or walnuts
¼ cup castor sugar
1 tablespoon water

Place sugar and water in a small saucepan and stir over low heat until sugar dissolves. Simmer gently until syrup changes to a golden brown. Watch very carefully that it does not burn. Place almonds in a lightly oiled cake tin or an oven tray. Immediately pour toffee over almonds and leave until set. Pulverise to a fine powder using a food processor fitted with a metal blade, or blender, or crush with a heavy object after placing Praline in a heavy plastic bag. Store in an air tight jar.

SUNDAES, COUPES, AND PARFAITS

Fruits, cakes, biscuits and liqueurs, combined with the numerous ice creams in this book and the sauces and toppings, create successful combinations called sundaes, coupes and parfaits.

Invent your own, keeping in mind, flavours, colours and textures which compliment each other.

GINGER BANANA SPLIT
Make 1 for each person

scoops of Ginger Chocolate Chip
  ice cream
banana
lemon juice
caramel sauce
Chantilly cream
chocolate curl

Place scoops of ice cream (see page 23) in the base of a long, shallow dish. Peel the banana and split in halves lengthwise. Rub over with lemon to prevent browning. Place halves around ice cream. Spoon over caramel sauce (see page 75), decorate with Chantilly cream (see page 72) and finish with a chocolate curl.

Serve immediately.

MOTHER'S SPECIAL
Make 1 for each person

vanilla ice cream, scoops
raspberry, strawberry or blackberry
  jam
bananas
cherry brandy
whipped cream
toasted chopped nuts

In the base of each sundae dish or glass, place a scoop of ice cream (see page 15), a teaspoon of jam and some sliced banana. Top with 2 teaspoons of brandy, a rosette of whipped cream and sprinkle with nuts. Accompany with a Meringue Finger (see page 83).

This rich and delightful combination of flavours is one which I was served by my mother as a child. Don't leave out the cherry brandy — it makes this dessert.

The ingredients in the following recipes are to be placed into serving dishes or goblets in the order they are listed.

Make 1 for each person

FANTASIA

Sponge cake cut into a disc to fit the base of a glass dish or goblet
(see page 63)
Cointreau, to taste
fresh fruits in season, chopped
scoop Vanilla Ice Cream
(see page 24)
champagne

Assemble the ingredients in the order they are listed. Finally pour over a little champagne at the table.

COCONUT PARFAIT

scoop of Coconut Ice Cream
(see page 21)
CocoRibe liqueur, to taste
Coconut Ice Cream
CocoRibe liqueur, to taste
whipped cream
grated orange rind
flaked almonds, toasted
maraschino cherry

Assemble in a long glass.

COUPE CHARTREUSE

scoop Vanilla Ice Cream
(see page 15)
green chartreuse, to taste
Dark Chocolate Sauce, hot
(see page 75)
Meringues, crumbled (see page 83)

PISTACHIO PEACH SUNDAE

scoop Pistachio Ice Cream
(see page 27)
whole peach, poached
(see page 82)
Strawberry Sauce (see page 72)
Langues de Chat biscuit
(see page 82)

PEAR RASPBERRY SUNDAE

Amaretti biscuits (Italian almond biscuits)
Raspberry Sherbet (see page 49)
pear halves, fresh or canned
whipped cream
chopped nuts

HOT APPLE SUNDAE

scoops of Honey Ice Cream
(see page 28)
canned pie apples
butter
cinnamon
sugar, optional
Calvados, optional

Heat pie apples in a small pan with butter, sugar and cinnamon and optional Calvados. Assemble sundae as soon as apples are heated through.

TUTTI FRUTTI

fresh fruit salad
Kirsch, to taste
scoops of Pineapple Ice Cream
(see page 58)
scoops of Strawberry Ice Cream
(see page 16)
scoops of Lemon Ice Cream
(see page 17)
1 slice of pineapple
glace cherry

VALENTINE

scoop Pistachio Ice Cream
(see page 27)
scoop Vanilla Ice Cream
(see page 15)
Chocolate Sauce (see page 75)
Chocolate Heart (see page 77)

COUPE BOHEMIENNE

scoop Vanilla Ice Cream
(see page 15)
Apricot Almond Sauce
(see page 72)
glace marrons (chestnuts)

COUPE ANGELO

crystallised fruit
Kirsch and Maraschino, to taste
scoop Lemon Ice Cream
(see page 17)
scoop Strawberry Ice Cream
(see page 16)
half peach
strawberry

Cut crystallised fruit into small pieces and marinate in Kirsch and Maraschino for one hour. Place in the bottom of coupe glasses. Fill up in the order of the ingredients finishing with the strawberry on top.

Photograph:
Centre. Pears Belle Helene (see recipe this page).
Front. Peach Melba (see recipe page 82).
Back. Strawberries Romanoff (see recipe page 82).

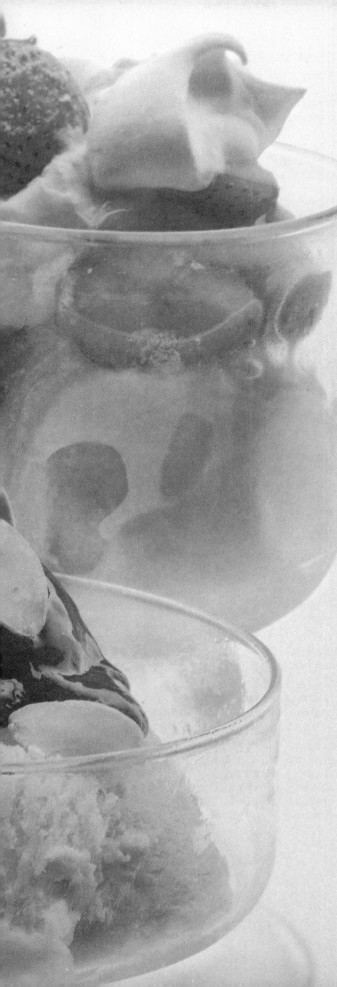

PINEAPPLE PRALINE PARFAIT

scoop Pineapple Ice Cream
    (see page 58)
Orange Sauce (see page 72)
Chantilly Cream (see page 72)
Praline (see page 78)

The next recipes are old time favourites with everyone. They will always be popular.

PEARS BELLE HELENE
Serves 4

4 large ripe pears
30 g unsalted butter
¼ cup almond meal
¼ cup icing sugar
500 ml vanilla ice cream
    (custard-based)
vanilla bean
1 teaspoon lemon juice
chocolate leaves
¾ cup sugar
2 cups water

Boil together ¾ cup sugar and 2 cups water to make a syrup. Peel the pears carefully leaving the stems intact. Core from the bottom without cutting through the stem end. Use an apple corer then dig out the core with a grapefruit knife. Immediately rub over the pears with the lemon juice. Split the vanilla bean in halves lengthwise to release the flavour and drop into the syrup. Gently poach the pears until tender, and cool in their syrup. Rinse the bean under cold water, pat dry on paper towels and store in castor sugar to make vanilla sugar. Soften the butter, mix in the sieved icing sugar and fold in the almond meal. Stuff into the hollowed pears. Make a Dark Chocolate Sauce (see page 75). Spread Custard-Based Vanilla Ice Cream (see page 37) into the base of a pretty bowl. Stand the pears upright on this and spoon over the sauce. Decorate with chocolate leaves (see page 77) and keep well chilled until ready for serving.

HILLIER'S INSPIRATION
Make 1 per person

vanilla ice cream, scoops
Hot Chocolate Sauce
Marshmallow Topping

Place scoops of ice cream (see page 24) in the bottom of a shallow dish. Spoon over Hot Fudge Sauce (see page 75). Immediately cap with spoons of Marshmallow Topping (see page 74).
Serve at once.

PEACH MELBA
Serves 4

2 large fresh peaches, or 4 canned
    peach halves
Custard-Based Vanilla Ice Cream
Melba Sauce
slivered almonds, toasted
4 teaspoons strawberry jam
2 cups water
¼ cup sugar

Make a syrup with the water and sugar,
stirring the mixture until it boils. Drop in the
fresh peaches and poach gently until tender.
While still hot, skin the peaches, then cool in
the cooking syrup. If using canned peaches,
don't cook them. Simply drain off syrup.
Place Custard-Based Vanilla Ice Cream (see
page 37) in four ice cream dishes or glass
goblets. Drop a teaspoon of jam on the ice
cream. Place the peach half, stone side
down, over the jam.

Spoon Melba Sauce (see page 73) over each
peach, covering them. Scatter over the
almonds and serve.

STRAWBERRIES ROMANOFF
Serves 4

125 g beautiful strawberries, or 1
    punnet
juice of 2 oranges
2 tablespoons Orange Curacao
rich vanilla ice cream
Chantilly Cream

Wipe over the strawberries with a damp cloth
if necessary. Reserve the four best
strawberries, hull the others and cut in halves
lengthwise if large, and macerate for several
hours in the orange juice and Orange
Curacao.

Scoop some Custard-Based Vanilla Ice
Cream into the base of four sundae glasses,
top with a tablespoon of strawberries, then
another scoop of ice cream. Top with
remaining fruit, a rosette of Chantilly Cream
(see page 72), and finally a strawberry
dipped into iced water then castor sugar.

All these classics require a good basic vanilla
ice cream. I've chosen the Custard-Based
Vanilla Ice Cream (see page 37) because it is
so easy to make and has a lovely creamy
texture. But the Vanilla Smoothy Ice Cream
(see page 15) will do equally well, and is not
as rich.

BANANA SPLIT
Make 1 for each person

scoops of Vanilla Ice Cream
banana
lemon juice
Chocolate sauce
Chantilly cream
toasted chopped nuts

Place scoops of vanilla ice cream (see page
15) in the base of a long dish. Peel the
banana and split in halves lengthwise. Rub
over with lemon to prevent browning. Place
halves either side of ice cream. Spoon over
Chocolate Sauce (see page 75), decorate
with rosettes of Chantilly Cream (see page
72) and scatter over almonds.

Serve with wafer biscuits.

ICE CREAM BISCUITS

It's nice to serve a little biscuit or meringue
with ice cream. They give a lovely change in
texture from the cold smooth ice cream to
the crunchy sweet biscuit. Several of these
recipes are for using left over egg whites. All
can be made in advance and they all store
well, if packed in airtight containers.

You should serve them separately on a pretty
plate, or at the side of individual serves.

LANGUES DE CHAT
Makes approximately 100

Make half the quantity for Tulipes (see page
59).

Set racks in the centre of the oven. Pre-heat
oven to 180°C (350°F). Butter and flour
several oven trays.

Place mixture into a piping bag fitted with a
1 cm plain tube. Pipe mixture into 8 cm
fingers, leaving plenty of space for
spreading.

Cook 4 minutes approximately or until the
biscuits are just beginning to turn golden
around the edges. Remove from trays with a
spatula and cool on a wire rack. Store in an
airtight container. They keep well for weeks,
if stored correctly. Serve with ice creams.

SPONGE FINGERS

½ cup plus 1 tablespoon icing
 sugar, sifted
⅔ cup castor sugar
1 cup flour, sifted
5 x 60 gm eggs
pinch of salt

Brush 2-3 baking trays with melted butter. Dust with flour, shaking off excess. Separate yolks and whites. Beat yolks with two-thirds of the castor sugar until pale and fluffy. Fold in flour and icing sugar. Beat whites with pinch of salt until soft peaks form. Gradually add the remaining castor sugar beating very well after each addition. Continue to beat whites until very firm but still glossy. Fold one-third of egg whites into yolk mixture then fold in remaining egg whites. Pile into a large piping bag fitted with a small star tube. Pipe sponge fingers, approximately 10 cm long, onto prepared trays. Sieve extra icing sugar over them.

Bake in the centre of a pre-heated oven 180°C (350°F) for about 15-20 minutes or until golden and firm. Cool on a wire rack and store in an airtight container.

CARAWAY SEED BUTTONS

Makes approximately 80

2 egg whites
pinch of salt
½ cup sugar
1 teaspoon carraway seeds

Beat egg whites with salt until soft peaks form. Continue to beat, adding sugar, 1 tablespoon at a time. Fold in the last two remaining tablespoons of sugar (don't beat) with the caraway seeds.

Preheat oven to 120°C (250°F) and lightly butter several trays.

Fit a piping bag with a 1 cm plain piping tube. Spoon the mixture into the bag and pipe 2½ cm buttons onto prepared baking trays.

Bake in the centre of the oven for one hour and five minutes approximately, or until meringues are dry but not brown. Cool on a wire rack and store in an airtight container.

These miniature meringues are delicious with all fruit-flavoured ice creams and sherbets, and can be used to "crown" the tops of ice creams or sundaes.

MERINGUE FINGERS

Use the base mixture for meringues (see page 83). To each egg white you need ¼ cup castor sugar and a few grains of salt. Prepare mixture as method in Carraway Seed Buttons (see page 83). Lightly butter oven trays and preheat oven to 120°C (250°F).

To make free-form meringue fingers: Place two heaped dessertspoonfuls at a time, on trays and make fingers approximately 10 cm long. Or, using a piping bag fitted with a 2 cm tube, pipe fingers approximately 10 cm long. Leave a space between each finger to allow for spreading. Cook in oven until dry but not brown, for approximately two hours.

COCONUT MACAROONS

Makes approximately 30

3 egg whites
1 cup castor sugar
2 cups desiccated coconut
2 teaspoons cornflour
vanilla flavouring

Beat egg whites until soft peaks form. Continue beating egg whites over hot water and beat in castor sugar, little by little, beating well after each addition. Fold in vanilla, then coconut and cornflour, using a rubber spatula. Place racks in the centre of the oven and preheat to 150°C (300°F). Cover oven trays with greaseproof paper and butter the paper lightly. Place mixture in heaped teaspoons on prepared trays and bake for approximately 30 minutes or until set.

Lift off paper with a spatula, cool on wire racks. When cold store airtight.

These macaroons are used in the Frozen Yoghurt or Ice Cream Trifle (see page 92). They are also excellent as an accompaniment to many ice creams and can be crushed and used as a topping for ice creams and sundaes, or folded through a fruity ice cream.

HOMEMADE YOGHURTS

Making your own yoghurt at home, is well worth while. It's less expensive than bought yoghurt and you benefit from the pure goodness of the ingredients.

Yoghurt-making calls for exactness, rather than skill and you don't need a machine to make it. If you carefully follow my instructions which are set out in clear steps, you will find it difficult to go wrong.

In the past two or three years, frozen yoghurt has become a dessert favourite. Frozen yoghurt has a texture between creamy ice cream and sherbet, with a tangy taste. It makes superb parfaits, grand iced desserts, sundaes and popsicles. Try it served in cones for nutritious after-school snacks.

But why just desserts? I've made breakfast yoghurts. Yes, frozen muesli yoghurt is wonderful on a hot summer's morning. There are some savoury ones too. Think of frozen tomato yoghurt as an appetiser, with freshly picked herbs snipped over it! And many more ideas as well. So join the yoghurt makers and be healthier for it.

WHERE YOGHURT BEGAN

The story of yoghurt began many thousands of years ago in the Middle East. The first yoghurt was made by accident. A nomad travelling with his camel, carried milk in a goatskin bag. The desert heat caused incubation which combined with the natural bacteria in the milk. At his destination he found, not milk, but an incredible thick custard with a tart taste.

So the use of yoghurt is not recent. It was used in early times for curing intestinal complaints as well as other ailments.

Today, there are many types of yoghurt and hundreds of flavours. And the latest fashion is frozen yoghurt. What a revelation!

Photographed:
Yoghurt with Fresh Herbs (see recipe page 90).

NUTRITION

Yoghurt is an excellent source of calcium, protein and riboflavin, and is a good supplement to a well-balanced diet.

What happens during yoghurt making:

During incubation, the bacteria in the yoghurt "starter" multiply, breaking up the sugar lactose in the milk or dairy product, to form lactic acid. This turns the milk or dairy product into the clotted, custard-like consistency which we call yoghurt.

WHAT CAN GO WRONG DURING YOGHURT MAKING:

If the yoghurt doesn't thicken:

1 The milk (dairy product) was too hot or too cold when added to the "starter".
2 Not enough "starter" was added.
3 The "starter" was too old and too weak.
4 The incubation temperature was too high or too low.
5 The yoghurt was disturbed during incubation.
6 Incubation time was too short.

If the yoghurt is too thin:

1 Not enough powdered milk or evaporated milk added to milk (dairy product). (None is needed in Smoothy yoghurt, it is rich enough on its own.)
2 Incubation time was too short.
3 "Starter" is too weak.

Too much moisture separation:

1 Incubation time was too long.
2 Yoghurt was moved during incubation.

If you read the instructions to successful yoghurt making, none of these problems should be experienced. It's really very easy once you know how.

SUCCESSFUL YOGHURT MAKING

Ingredients:

1 Dairy products, see notes on page 6. Homogenized milk in cartons is not covered in those notes. It is the best choice for milk yoghurt as the cream has been distributed throughout the milk and therefore produces a smooth-textured yoghurt with no cream separation. I have used bottled milk successfully too, but you will have a skin on the yoghurt as the cream has not been pre-distributed.
2 "Starter" culture, is the most important ingredient for yoghurt-making. Begin with a commercially-made, natural, non-pasteurized yoghurt. It must be fresh. Store it in the refrigerator. Buy it

from a reliable vendor, health food stores usually stock natural yoghurts and have a good turn over of fresh stock. After fourteen days, don't use it for "starter". Save a couple of tablespoons from homemade yoghurt to "start" the next batch. "Starter" must not be flavoured or contain gelatine. After a couple of weeks the bacteria in the yoghurt becomes weak or inactive and it is therefore not suitable to use as a "starter". Begin again, with fresh commercial yoghurt.

To test if "starter" is strong enough, stir two tablespoons of yoghurt at room temperature into a cup of milk warmed to 45°C (113°F). Incubate (see notes on incubation), and leave undisturbed, preferably overnight. If the milk sets to a thickish consistency, the yoghurt is still active and therefore is still suitable for "starter".

3 Flavourings for yoghurts are similar to those for ice creams.
4 Gelatine, is used in flavoured yoghurts to make the consistency firmer. Some flavourings make the yoghurt rather thin. See notes on how to use gelatine.

EQUIPMENT NECESSARY FOR SUCCESSFUL YOGHURT MAKING

Most kitchens will already have these utensils, except maybe a thermometer which registers as low as 45°C (113°F). You will need one for heating the milk or dairy product to the correct degree. They come in a range of prices. An expensive thermometer is not necessary.

You will also need a saucepan, measuring spoon and jug, whisk, small bowl and either jars or thermos flasks.

The basic requirement is an apparatus which will maintain a constant, low temperature for growing the culture. This process is called incubation.

INCUBATORS:

A yoghurt maker. There are several types and many makes, with varying capacities and prices to choose from.

Thermos flasks. These make ideal incubators, and most people will already own one or two.

Electric frying pan, skillet or saucepan. Set on approximately no. 1 or a temperature of 45°C (113°F) and covered with a blanket.

Baking dish. Filled with water heated to the incubating temperature of 45°C and covered with blankets.

There is too much room for mistakes in the last two methods. I prefer the thermos flask method which I find delightfully simple.

If you've never made yoghurt before, read through my notes before beginning. It will pay dividends.

HOW TO MAKE PLAIN HOMEMADE YOGHURT

1 Take "starter" yoghurt from your refrigerator and let come to room temperature.

2 Sterilize every utensil itemised in the equipment list by pouring boiling water over them. Leave one minute and pour off. Don't wipe dry, simply drain. (Place a metal spoon in glass jars to prevent breakage.)

3 Choose the yoghurt recipe you wish to make. There are three basic yoghurts to choose from, see page 89.

4 If using a yoghurt maker, switch it on. Having chosen the type of yoghurt you wish to make, mix the dairy product and milk powder or evaporated milk in the saucepan with a whisk. Heat gently with the thermometer standing in it.

5 Measure the "starter" yoghurt into the bowl and stir with the whisk until creamy.

6 Watch the dairy product carefully, it must not get too hot. Heat until thermometer reads 45°C (113°F). If you overheat it, wait until it cools to the correct temperature.

7 Immediately pour half a cup of the heated dairy product onto the "starter" and mix well stirring with the whisk. Pour back into pan and mix thoroughly.

8 Immediately pour into thermos flasks or incubating jars. If using flasks, screw down tops, cap and leave in a quiet place to incubate. If using a yoghurt maker, follow the maker's instructions.

9 Leave, completely undisturbed for at least four hours. Test, by shaking gently to see if the yoghurt is lightly set. At this stage, the yoghurt is still slightly "sweet". Cover and leave to incubate longer if you like a tarter taste or if you want it thicker. See recipes on plain yoghurts for expected results, pages 89-90.

10 When firm, refrigerate for three to four hours before serving. If leaving in the thermos flasks, remove lids, cover with plastic wrap or foil and refrigerate.

STORAGE: Yoghurt should be stored, covered in the refrigerator for approximately two weeks for plain, and one week for flavoured. If there is condensation on the top of the yoghurt or if there is any moisture separation, either blot with paper towels or stir into yoghurt.

FLAVOURING: "Sweet" or tart yoghurt. If the dairy product is added to the "starter" at 45°C (113°F) the taste will be determined by the length of the incubation. The shorter the incubation time the "sweeter" the yoghurt. A longer incubation, for instance over night, results in fairly tart yoghurt.

TO MAKE FLAVOURED YOGHURT:

Before incubation: Place flavourings according to recipe chosen in the bottom of the thermos flasks or incubating jars, and continue as for plain yoghurt.

After incubation: Stir in chosen flavourings and dissolved gelatine, and leave refrigerated to develop flavours and to set loosely.

You will notice that the flavoured yoghurts in this book all have the flavourings added after incubation. I like to have plain yoghurt on hand, it's the most versatile and becomes my sub-culture, or "starter" for my next batch of yoghurt making. It keeps longer than flavoured. Remember that homemade yoghurt doesn't have any preservatives.

Flavourings added before incubation tend to sink to the bottom.

HOW TO MAKE FROZEN YOGHURT

Process in the same manner as ice cream. The various methods are discussed on pages 6-13 under How To Make Ice Cream. There are four methods discussed. All are suitable for freezing yoghurt. It should then be covered and left to ripen in the freezer for one to two hours.

Frozen yoghurt is best eaten the day it is made. It stores well for approximately two weeks. Before serving, stand in the lower part of the refrigerator for one hour to soften slightly.

YOGHURTS

Here they are. Wonderful, tempting, homemade yoghurts!

There are three basic yoghurts, with a host of recipe ideas to follow and flavours to enjoy. Some yoghurts you can buy at the supermarket, but once you've tasted the difference and found just how easy it is, and economical too; you will be won over like me.

Try frozen yoghurts — the new taste sensation. Scooped into cones they make luscious licks for healthy after-school snacks.

WHOLE MILK YOGHURT

This is a good basic yoghurt with a firm set almost like junket. It is excellent for flavouring and freezing.

SMOOTHY YOGHURT

Smoothy makes a rich yoghurt with a slight top skin of cream. It's an excellent yoghurt for all beverages, malts and shakes.

SKINNY YOGHURT

This makes a low fat yoghurt which is very good for slimmers and anyone on a special diet. Skinny yoghurt is white, very firm and an ideal base for the yoghurt drinks and iced soup recipes.

Photograph:
Front. Frozen Tomato Yoghurt (see recipe page 91).
Back. Vegetable Juice Sherbet (see recipe page 51).

PLAIN WHOLE MILK YOGHURT
Makes 1 litre (4 cups) approximately

1 litre (4 cups) plain whole milk
¼ cup full cream or skim milk powder
2 tablespoons fresh yoghurt.

Rinse all the utensils necessary for making yoghurt in boiling water to sterilise them.

Pour milk into saucepan and blend in milk powder. Heat to 45°C (113°F) and immediately remove from heat. Break up yoghurt with a whisk in a small bowl, and pour in half a cup of the heated enriched milk. Blend well and return to the saucepan.

Pour into sterilised jars or thermos flasks. Cover and leave to incubate for four to six hours, completely undisturbed. After that time, check to see if mixture is firm, by shaking it gently. Leave for another hour or two if not firm enough.
Refrigerate (uncovered, if in thermos flasks).

PLAIN SMOOTHY YOGHURT
Makes 1 litre (4 cups)

500 ml (2 cups) Smoothy
500 ml (2 cups) whole milk
3 tablespoons fresh yoghurt

To sterilise the yoghurt-making utensils: Pour boiling water over the thermometer, measuring spoon and whisk, into a large saucepan, a small mixing bowl and the thermos flasks or incubating jars.

Pour milk and Smoothy into the saucepan, mix well with the sterilised whisk and insert thermometer. Heat gently to 45°C (113°F) and remove from heat immediately.

Measure the "starter" yoghurt into the mixing bowl and break up with the whisk. While the milk and Smoothy still read 45°C pour a small amount onto the starter and blend using the whisk. Stir yoghurt milk mixture into combined Smoothy and milk, blend well and pour into thermos flasks or incubating jars. Cover and incubate for four to six hours or overnight. Do not disturb during incubation.

After four hours, remove lids and gently shake mixture to see if it is set. If not, cover again and leave another one to two hours.

Yoghurt should be refrigerated as soon as it is set. Remove the thermos lids and refrigerate in the open thermos flasks. Avoid disturbing the yoghurt which will make it thin. If using a yoghurt maker, store in incubating jars, with the lids on.

PLAIN SKINNY YOGHURT
Makes ¾ litre (3 cups)

500 ml (2 cups) Skinny
¾ cup low fat evaporated milk
2 tablespoons fresh yoghurt

Sterilise all the utensils for making yoghurt with boiling water.

Heat Skinny and evaporated milk together in a saucepan to 45°C (113°F) and immediately remove from heat.

Mix yoghurt in a small bowl until creamy, pour on half a cup of the heated milks and blend. Return to the saucepan and pour into sterilised thermos flasks or incubating jars. Cover and leave, undisturbed for four to six hours or until set.

Refrigerate (uncovered, if in thermos flasks).

YOGHURT WITH FRESH HERBS
Serves 4

500 ml (2 cups) plain yoghurt
salt to taste
1 teaspoon gelatine, mixed with 3
   tablespoons hot water
2 teaspoons fresh tarragon, finely
   chopped
2 teaspoons fresh parsley, finely
   chopped
1 teaspoon fresh chives, finely
   snipped
Garnish:
radishes
cucumber
extra tarragon sprigs

Fold herbs through yoghurt with gelatine and salt. Prepare 4 small moulds, approximately 125 ml (½ cup) capacity, and coat the insides using a brush which has been dipped in egg white. Spoon yoghurt mixture into prepared moulds and leave to set in the refrigerator. Turn out of moulds on to serving plate, garnish with cucumber and radish fans, which have been chilled in iced water.

Serve chilled as an appetiser or a palate refresher after the main course.

I used French coeur a la creme moulds, which are traditionally heart-shaped and have holes in the bottom. This is to drain the whey from the curds in the classic heart of cream recipe. To prevent my yoghurt escaping through the holes, I plugged them with match sticks.

VANILLA YOGHURT
Serves 4

500 ml (2 cups) Plain yoghurt
castor sugar, to taste
vanilla flavouring
1 teaspoon gelatine, mixed with 3
   tablespoons hot water

Stir into yoghurt with sugar and vanilla to taste. Refrigerate for several hours.

Instead of castor sugar and vanilla flavouring, vanilla sugar can be used. It's cheaper to make your own vanilla sugar. Split a vanilla bean in halves lengthwise and store in an airtight jar buried in castor sugar.

RAW VEGETABLE YOGHURT
Serves 6

500 ml (2 cups) plain yoghurt
1 medium carrot, grated
1 medium cucumber, grated with
   skin
6 red radishes, grated
2 teaspoons mint, finely chopped
celery salt, to taste
1 teaspoon gelatine, mixed with 3
   tablespoons hot water

Sprinkle salt over grated carrot and cucumber and leave with a plate weighted on top for half an hour.

Drain juices from salted vegetables and fold through yoghurt with all the other ingredients. Chill for several hours. Serve in small lettuce leaves or piled into scooped out tomato cases as a first course.

Zucchini, celery, spring onions and other garden vegetables all finely chopped or grated make a pleasant change to this interesting and refreshing yoghurt.

CHOCOLATE YOGHURT
Serves 4-5

500 ml (2 cups) plain yoghurt
125 g cooking chocolate

Grate 2 tablespoons of the chocolate and break the rest into squares. Melt squares in a small pan over hot water stirring from time to time with a wooden spoon until melted. Cool a little and stir into yoghurt, straight from the incubator or at room temperature. (If the yoghurt is too cold the chocolate will solidify in it before it is properly mixed). Chill until ready to serve. Present with grated chocolate over each serving.

BANANA HONEY YOGHURT
Serves 5-6

500 ml (2 cups) plain yoghurt
2 ripe bananas, medium sized
¼ cup brown sugar, or to taste
2 tablespoons honey
vanilla flavouring
1 teaspoon gelatine, mixed with 3
   tablespoons hot water

Mash bananas and fold through yoghurt with other ingredients. Taste and adjust if necessary. Refrigerate for several hours before serving.

PEACH YOGHURT
Serves 5-6

500 ml (2 cups) plain yoghurt
1 cup fresh or canned peaches,
   drained
½ cup brown sugar, or to taste
almond flavouring
1 teaspoon gelatine, mixed with 3
   tablespoons hot water

Mash peach flesh or chop very finely and stir into yoghurt with other ingredients. Leave to chill in the refrigerator for a few hours before serving.

HONEY APPLE YOGHURT
Serves 6

500 ml (2 cups) plain yoghurt
1 cup bought apple sauce
2 tablespoons honey, or to taste
pinch cloves
pinch cinnamon
green food colouring, optional
1 teaspoon gelatine, mixed with 3
   tablespoons hot water

Stir into yoghurt with remaining ingredients and colour a pretty green. Chill for several hours before serving.

COFFEE YOGHURT
Serves 5

500 ml (2 cups) plain yoghurt
2 tablespoons instant coffee powder,
   mixed with 2 tablespoons warm
   water
½ cup sugar, or to taste
1 teaspoon gelatine, mixed with 3
   tablespoons hot water

Stir all ingredients together and chill several hours before serving.

BERRY YOGHURT
Serves 5

500 ml (2 cups) plain yoghurt
1 cup berries, fresh or frozen
½ cup sugar, or to taste
1 teaspoon gelatine, mixed with 3
   tablespoons hot water

Crush berries with a fork or potato masher and fold into yoghurt with other ingredients. Leave in the refrigerator for a few hours before serving.

Any berries which don't need cooking make an easy berry yoghurt.

DRIED APRICOT YOGHURT
Serves 4-5

500 ml (2 cups) plain yoghurt
12 dried apricots, chopped finely
1 tablespoon sugar, or to taste
pinch ground cloves
1 teaspoon gelatine, mixed with 3
   tablespoons hot water

Mix all ingredients together and taste. Adjust sweetness if necessary. Refrigerate for several hours before serving.

For Apricot Orange Yoghurt, use this recipe but add 2 tablespoons finely grated orange rind. For Apricot Pistachio Yoghurt, add ½ cup skinned pistachios roughly chopped to this recipe.

FROZEN TOMATO YOGHURT
Serves 4

500 ml (2 cups) plain yoghurt
3 large ripe tomatoes
1 teaspoon salt
⅛ teaspoon pepper
1 teaspoon Worcestershire sauce
6 drops Tabasco
1 teaspoon sugar
1 teaspoon gelatine, mixed with 3
   tablespoons hot water

Blanch the tomatoes in boiling water for approximately 30 seconds. Remove the skins. Remove cores and cut in halves horizontally. Squeeze the seeds out into a strainer and catch the juice which should measure approximately half a cup. Discard the seeds. Chop the flesh medium-fine. Stir gelatine into yoghurt with all other ingredients, including the half cup of tomato juice. Chill. Either churn or set by the freeze/beat method. Cover and ripen in the freezer for one hour, or until firm.

FROZEN YOGHURT TRIFLE
Serves 10

3½ cups vanilla or strawberry
  yoghurt
2 jam rollettes, from a packet of 6
13-16 lady finger biscuits
6 tablespoons strawberry jam
4 tablespoons sherry, port or brandy
2 tablespoons water
60 g coconut macaroons
Garnish:
150 ml thickened cream
castor sugar to taste
whole hazelnuts
angelica leaves

Line the bottom of an 18 cm charlotte
mould with sliced jam rollettes, packing
them tightly but placing in an attractive
pattern. Mix the sherry, port or brandy with 2
tablespoons water and place in a shallow
dish. Dip sponge fingers into mixture and
line sides of mould, facing the flat sides of the
fingers outwards. Put them as closely
together as possible. Ladle a cup of yoghurt
over the base. Spoon half the jam over the
yoghurt, then crush half the macaroons over
the jam. Repeat this layer beginning with

another cup of yoghurt and ending with the remaining macaroons. Top with remaining yoghurt and smooth over the top to give a flat finish. Cover with foil and freeze until firm.

To unmould, dip into warm water, invert on a serving plate and shake out. Lift off mould.

To decorate as in photograph on this page. Whip the cream and sweeten slightly. Spoon into a forcing bag fitted with a small star tube, pipe small rosettes down the sides of the trifle between the sponge fingers. Place a hazelnut in the centre of each rosette.

Decorate around the top of the trifle in the same manner, giving each cream rosette a pair of angelica leaves.

This trifle is lovely made with apricot yoghurt, in which case apricot jam replaces strawberry jam.

Angelica is obtained more easily around Christmas time, when it is more in demand, but some health food stores stock it all year round. Most commercial angelicas are celery, dyed green, which look pretty but do not have the flavour of true angelica.

Photograph:
Frozen Yoghurt Trifle (see recipe this page).

FROZEN RASPBERRY YOGHURT
Serves 5

500 ml (2 cups) plain yoghurt
125 g raspberries, fresh or frozen
⅔ cup sugar
1 teaspoon lemon juice
1 egg
vanilla flavouring

Poach raspberries with sugar until sugar dissolves and fruit softens, about four minutes. Cool and stir in lemon juice and vanilla. Separate the egg, beat the yolk into the fruit mixture and fold through yoghurt. Beat the white until soft peaks form and fold into mixture. Chill.

Either churn or set by the freeze/beat method. Cover and ripen one to two hours, or until firm, before serving. Spoon into individual glass dishes, garnish with a sprig of fresh mint and serve with a wafer biscuit.

A change is always welcome, so why not try this recipe with other berries?

FROZEN CHERRY YOGHURT
Serves 4

500 ml (2 cups) plain yoghurt
5 tablespoons cherry conserve
1 teaspoon gelatine, mixed with 3 tablespoons hot water

Mix all ingredients together and chill. Churn or set by the freeze/beat method. Cover and ripen for one to two hours, or until firm, before serving.

This is good with Morello Cherry Sauce (see page 74) or cherry brandy spooned over the top.

Practically any jam, jelly or conserve can be substituted for cherry conserve. Always taste the mixture before setting it, remembering that a cold dish needs a sharper flavour, so the mixture must have a strong taste before freezing.

FROZEN PLUM YOGHURT
Serves 5

500 ml (2 cups) plain yoghurt
6 plums (red, yellow or blood plums)
⅔ cup sugar
½ cup water
1 teaspoon gelatine, mixed with 3 tablespoons hot water
Chantilly cream
flaked almonds, toasted

Cut plums in halves and remove stones. Cook gently with sugar and water until tender. Puree and cool. Fold gelatine through yoghurt. Chill. Churn or set by the freeze/beat method. Cover and ripen in the freezer for one to two hours, or until firm .

Scoops of plum yoghurt are delicious garnished with Chantilly cream and toasted almond flakes. (See cream recipe page 72.)

FROZEN FRUIT PUDDING
Serves 4

250 ml (1 cup) plain yoghurt
¼ cup raisins, softened in warm water
¼ cup glace cherries, chopped
¼ cup slivered almonds, toasted
¼ cup crushed pineapple, drained
⅓ cup icing sugar, sifted
2 egg whites.

Drain sultanas, stir into yoghurt with remaining fruits, nuts and sugar. Beat egg whites until they form soft peaks. Fold into yoghurt mixture and pour into a small freezer container or a 2½ cup mould rinsed out with cold water. Cover and freeze until firm.

If using a mould, dip into warm water invert over a serving plate shake out pudding and serve. If too hard, leave on the bottom shelf of refrigerator for half an hour before serving.

FROZEN ALMOND YOGHURT
Serves 4-5

500 ml (2 cups) plain yoghurt
1 cup blanched almonds, toasted
   and finely ground
1 cup soft brown sugar
almond flavouring
1 teaspoon gelatine, mixed with 3
   tablespoons hot water

Combine all the ingredients and taste. Adjust if necessary. Chill, then churn or set by the freeze/beat method. Cover and ripen one to two hours, or until firm, before serving.

Try frozen almond yoghurt served with coffee or chocolate yoghurt spooned over the top.

FROZEN MUESLI YOGHURT
Serves 3

250 ml (1 cup) plain yoghurt
1 cup containing muesli
        peanuts, chopped
        bran
        lecathin
        dried apricots,
        chopped or sultanas
1 tablespoon clear honey

Fold all ingredients together, pour into a small container, cover and freeze for 2-3 hours or until firm.

Serve icy-cold for breakfast on a hot summer's day or as a snack scooped into a cone, or sandwiched between 2 wafers.

FROZEN RASPBERRY MACAROON YOGHURT
Serves 6

500 ml (2 cups) plain yoghurt
1 cup raspberries, fresh or frozen
½ cup sugar
½ cup crushed macaroons
1 teaspoon lemon juice
1 egg
vanilla flavouring

Make as for Frozen Raspberry Yoghurt (see page 94) folding in Coconut Macaroons (see page 83) just before the mixture sets.

YOGHURT CASSATA
Serves 10-12

2 cups frozen peppermint crisp
   yoghurt
1½ cups frozen almond yoghurt
1 cup frozen raspberry macaroon
   yoghurt
2 slices glace pineapple, chopped
2 glace apricots, chopped
4 green glace cherries, chopped
2 tablespoons sultanas
2 tablespoons Kirsch or rum

Choose a 6-cup pudding basin and paint the inside with egg white. Place in the freezer. Macerate the fruits in the alcohol.

Prepare Frozen Peppermint Crisp Yoghurt (see page 97) and when nearly set, spread 2 cups around inside of the well-chilled pudding basin leaving a hollowed out centre for the next two layers of yoghurt. If this proves difficult (which it can in hot weather) build up this first layer of yoghurt in stages, letting each stage set before adding the next. Leave to harden in the freezer.

While the first layer is setting prepare the Frozen Almond Yoghurt (see this page). When nearly set, spread 1½ cups over the first layer, hollowing out the centre for the final flavour. Cover and freeze until firm.

Finally prepare the frozen raspberry macaroon yoghurt. When it is almost set, fold through the macerated fruits and pile into the centre of the basin. Level the top of the yoghurts with a spatula, cover and freeze, preferably overnight.

To serve: dip basin in warm water, invert on a serving plate and shake out. This is easier said than done, because you have to release the vacuum of air in the basin. Lots of patience and several dippings later, the cassata will eventually drop out, usually when you least expect it!

So, do be patient, and don't dig it out (you will mark it) and don't increase the heat, or you will melt it — it's worth it, you will see.

If the cassata has melted around the edges, return to the freezer to firm. If it is too hard to serve, soften in the lower part of the refrigerator for half an hour before serving, cut into wedges.

You can line the basin with foil but the wrinkles dent the yoghurt, and since cassata has no icing or coverings, it looks terrible.

FROZEN MANGO YOGHURT
Serves 4-5

500 ml (2 cups) plain yoghurt
200 g mango puree
1 teaspoon gelatine, mixed with 3
    tablespoons hot water
2 teaspoons lemon juice
crystallised orange rind

Mix all ingredients together, except rind, and chill. Churn or set by the freeze/beat method. Cover and ripen in the freezer for one to two hours, or until firm, before serving.

Using a vegetable peeler, pare rind off an orange (rind only, no white pith). Cut into fine matchsticks. Alternately, use a marmalade shredder. Blanch rind in boiling water for 1 minute, drain and toss in castor sugar, and use to garnish.

A wonderful fruity yoghurt which is excellent for breakfast. Try topping it with lecathin or toasted muesli.

There are good brands of mango pulp or puree available, which are often cheaper in the southern states than the fresh fruit.

Photographed L. to R.
Frozen Mango Yoghurt
Frozen Pineapple Yoghurt
Frozen Peppermint Crisp Yoghurt
(see all recipes this page).

FROZEN PINEAPPLE YOGHURT
Serves 5

500 ml (2 cups) plain yoghurt
½ of 450 g can crushed pineapple
2 teaspoons gelatine, mixed with 3
  tablespoons hot water

Fold all ingredients together and chill. Either churn or set by the freeze/beat method. Cover and ripen in the freezer for one to two hours, or until firm, before serving.

Scoops of frozen pineapple yoghurt are enhanced with crushed Peanut Crackle (see page 76) or toasted flaked almonds, on top.

There are many complimentary flavours which go well with this frozen yoghurt. Raspberry or strawberry sauce are wonderful, and a fresh fruit salad made with orange segments and slices of Kiwi fruit is tangy and attractive.

FROZEN PEPPERMINT CRISP YOGHURT
Serves 4

500 ml (2 cups) plain yoghurt
90 g peppermint crisps (3 crisps)
Peppermint essence, to taste
Green food colouring, optional
1 teaspoon gelatine, mixed with 3
  tablespoons hot water

Crush Peppermint Crisps in a plastic bag with a rolling pin or other heavy object, and fold through yoghurt with other ingredients. Chill and churn or set by the freeze/beat method. Cover and ripen one to two hours, or until firm.

Extra Peppermint Crisps, crushed and served over the top give added flavour and texture.

FROZEN FIG YOGHURT
Serves 5

500 ml (2 cups) plain yoghurt
200 g ripe rigs, purple or white
½ cup sugar
1 teaspoon gelatine, mixed with 3
tablespoons hot water

Peel figs, chop roughly and cook with sugar over gentle heat, stirring until sugar dissolves. Simmer very slowly for 10 minutes, then puree. Fold in gelatine and leave to cool. Stir yoghurt into fig mixture and chill. Either churn or set by the freeze/beat method. Cover and ripen in the freezer until firm.

FROZEN PRUNE YOGHURT
Serves 5

500 ml (2 cups) plain yoghurt
10 dried prunes
juice of 1 orange
2 cloves
¾ cup soft brown sugar
1 teaspoon gelatine, mixed with 3
tablespoons hot water

Stone prunes and cook in orange juice with cloves until tender. Discard cloves and puree prunes, or chop very finely. Stir gelatine into puree with sugar and yoghurt. Chill.

Churn the mixture or set by the freeze/beat method. Cover and ripen for one to two hours, or until firm, before serving.

Try serving this yoghurt with Orange Sauce (see page 72).

Whenever you cook prunes, include a few cloves, they enhance the flavour considerably.

FRUITY YOGHURT SAUCE
Makes 1¼ cups approximately

250 ml (1 cup) vanilla yoghurt
2 tablespoons honey
1 teaspoon lemon juice
1 tablespoon orange juice
concentrate

Whisk honey into the yoghurt and add lemon juice and orange juice concentrate.

Spoon over fresh fruits or fruit salad and serve.

SUMMER SOUP
Serves 4

500 ml (2 cups) plain yoghurt
1 cup Skinny
1 green cucumber
8 red radishes
2 tablespoons spring onions,
chopped finely
2 teaspoons salt
½ teaspoon white pepper
garnish:
2 teaspoons fresh dill, snipped finely
4 baby sprigs fresh mint

Wipe over cucumber, top and tail radishes and grate them both on a medium-fine grater. Stir into yoghurt and Skinny with remaining ingredients except garnishes. Mix well and chill. Chill soup bowls too. When ready to serve ladle into bowls and sprinkle over dill. Garnish with sprigs of mint.

This most attractive pale soup with flecks of green and red through it is light, refreshing and tangy. A very good starter to a rich meal. An excellent luncheon dish accompanied with buttered fingers of light rye or fairy toast and also an excellent slimmer's dish.

BANANA YOGHURT THICK SHAKE
Serves 1

250 ml (1 cup) plain yoghurt
1 scoop ice cream
2 tablespoons raw sugar
1 ripe banana, medium size

Blend all ingredients together in a blender and serve in a long glass. An alternative method to making this drink with a blender would be to mash the banana with a fork, place in a hand held milkshake-shaker with the remaining three ingredients and shake until frothy. Serve at once.

TOMATO SUPREME YOGHURT
Serves 4

500 ml (2 cups) plain yoghurt
1 x 310 g can tomato supreme
1 teaspoon Worcestershire sauce
1 teaspoon gelatine, mixed with 3
    tablespoons hot water

Stir gelatine into tomato supreme and mix in all remaining ingredients. Refrigerate for several hours or until lightly set.

This is a delicious yoghurt served at either breakfast, lunch or dinner.

Served in crisp lettuce cups and accompanied with fresh young garden vegetables. It makes a pleasant luncheon dish.

BREAKFAST COOLER
Serves 2-3

500 ml (2 cups) plain yoghurt
2 teaspoons wheatgerm
1 cup pineapple juice, apricot nectar,
    orange juice or juice of your
    choice, chilled
2 tablespoons honey

Blend or shake all ingredients until frothy. Serve at once in long glasses.

This is an excellent drink for breakfast on a hot summer's day. It can be made and served in one glass and is therefore very quick. It's easily digested as well as being healthy and nutritious.

BANANA ORANGE CREAM
Serves 4

4 ripe bananas, medium sized
500 ml (2 cups) plain yoghurt
1 tablespoon finely grated orange
    rind
1 tablespoon castor sugar
garnish:
desiccated coconut, toasted
dark chocolate, grated finely

Blend banana yoghurt and sugar together until almost smooth. Leave some banana chunks in the cream, it makes it more interesting. Fold through grated orange rind. Pour into 4 tall glass dishes. Cover and chill. Just before serving garnish with a little coconut and chocolate. Serve accompanied by a small biscuit (see pages 82 and 83).

WALNUT YOGHURT SAUCE
Makes 1½ cups approximately

250 ml (1 cup) plain yoghurt
1 clove garlic
1 tablespoon olive oil
¼ cup walnut pieces
3 teaspoons cider vinegar or white
    wine vinegar
salt to taste
2 tablespoons parsley, finely
    chopped

Blend garlic, walnuts, olive oil and vinegar together. Stir into yoghurt with parsley and salt to taste, mixing very well. Serve in a glass dish in the centre of a platter surrounded with fresh crisp young vegetables and pickled vegetables, such as gherkins, olives etc.

If you don't have a blender then you should chop the garlic and walnuts very finely and stir all the ingredients together.

This variation on a classic Greek sauce is excellent with mixed vegetables, deep fried.

RASPBERRY YOGHURT FOOL
Serves 4

1¼ cups plain yoghurt
250 g raspberries, fresh or frozen
1 tablespoon castor sugar, or to taste
1 tablespoon Kirsch

Blend all ingredients together until smooth and creamy. Taste and adjust the sugar if necessary. Pour into 4 glass dishes. Cover and chill until ready to serve.

At the time of serving an extra dessertspoon of yoghurt can be swirled into the top of each dessert, using a fork, to leave a marbled effect. Serve with a little biscuit (see pages 82 and 83).

Raspberries can be substituted by any other berries which don't require cooking.

If using frozen berries, they must be thawed first and the juices used in the Fool with the fruit.

EGGYOG
Serves 1

250 ml (1 cup) plain yoghurt
1 egg
2 tablespoons brown sugar
2 tablespoons Advokaat, liqueur
nutmeg

Blend or shake all ingredients together except nutmeg until frothy. Pour into long glass, sprinkle nutmeg over the top.

MILK

For centuries men have domesticated animals in order to milk them. Over two hundred years of scientific rearing have produced herds of dairy cows capable of a large milk yield. Goats, and in some countries camels, buffaloes, reindeer, asses, mares and other animals are also milked.

However, it is cow's milk we are concerned with in this book. The products of milk are many today, but those which form the basis for this collection of recipes, are described on page 6.

Milk is the most complete food we know, containing nearly every type of nutrient.

It should be stored in the refrigerator and away from direct light which can destroy its vitamin B content.

Australian milk is pasteurised to kill bacteria, without destroying any of the nutrients. It's for this reason that I don't recommend boiling our milk or dairy products in yoghurt-making. It is totally unneccessary.

EQUIPMENT

For making dairy drinks quickly and easily, the simplest utensils will suffice. A rotary beater or whisk is useful. A blender or food processor will give excellent results, and there are milk-shake makers made by several manufacturers. I found an inexpensive hand held shaker was very successful for mixing most of these drinks. It's called a Turbot shaker. It consists of a plastic beaker with a capacity of 1¼ cups, and a tight fitting lid with special, curved, vanes on the inverted cones at the base and inside the lid. These propel the contents around inside to integrate effectively. You can see through it, which is sensible because you know immediately your drink is blended and frothy. You can even drink right out of the shaker if you hate washing up as much as I do!

Photograph:
Jug. Stamina Milk Shake
Glass. Breakfast On The Run
(see recipes page 102).

101

DAIRY DRINKS

The versatility of milk and milk products is shown in the wide range of drinks based on milk. From Skinny Thick Shakes to Creamy Cocktails, and Healthy Breakfast Drinks to Piping Hot Toddies. There's something here for everyone.

STAMINA MILKSHAKE
Makes 2 drinks

500 ml Skinny
sugar or sugar substitute, to taste
1 tablespoon safflower oil
vanilla flavouring
3 tablespoons powdered yeast
4 tablespoons lecathin

Blend all ingredients together in a blender or food processor, or beat with a rotary beater. Leave refrigerated overnight to dissipate the yeast flavour. Next day, blend again or beat until foamy and serve in long glasses.

BREAKFAST-ON-THE-RUN
Makes 1 drink

1 cup milk
juice of 1 orange
1 egg
2 teaspoons honey
2 teaspoons wheatgerm

Blend all ingredients together in a blender, food processor or rotary beater. Serve chilled in a long glass.

A quick, easy and nutritious breakfast drink.

For the busy person in a hurry, this is no more than five minutes work, from starting the preparation, drinking it, and cleaning up afterwards. Try to make it in the gless you intend to drink it from — that way you only have the glass, spoon, juicer and beater to wash up!

BANANA HONEY EGG FLIP
Makes 1 drink

1 cup milk, chilled
1 egg
1 banana
2 teaspoons honey

Beat or whisk all ingredients together, preferably right in the glass, and drink while frothy.

COOPER'S SPECIAL
Makes 1 long drink

300 ml Big Iced Coffee M, chilled
Brandy

Pour Big M into a long glass, stir in brandy to taste. Enjoy it, instead of a beer!
A recipe from the ideas man of "Milk it Instead" fame.

BIG BANANA — HONEY MALTED
Makes 1 long drink

300 ml Big Banana M
2 teaspoons honey
2 teaspoons malt milk powder
1 scoop vanilla, banana, or honey ice cream

Blend all ingredients together until frothy. Serve chilled in a long glass with a straw.

MARSALA EGG FLIP
Makes 1 drink

1 cup Smoothy, chilled
¼ cup Marsala
1 egg
½ teaspoon vanilla essence
2 teaspoons sugar
cinnamon

Beat all ingredients together except cinnamon. Pour into long glass. Sprinkle cinnamon over the top.

MIXED FRUIT WHIP
Makes 2 long drinks

500 ml milk, chilled
½ banana
1 apricot
8 strawberries
juice of 1 orange
2 teaspoons sugar
6 ice cubes
2 tablespoons Maraschino

Stone apricot and chop roughly. Skin banana and chop roughly. Hull strawberries and add all fruit to milk in a blender, with juice, Maraschino, ice and sugar. Blend until smooth and frothy. Serve in long glasses.

Other fruits, such as peaches, grapes and nectarines, and all the berry fruits could be substituted for those used.

If you don't have a blender, chop all the fruits very fine or crush with a potato masher. Shake all ingredients together.

BIG CARAMEL MARSHMALLOW
Makes 1 long drink

300 ml Big Caramel M
¼ cup marshmallow topping
1 scoop vanilla ice cream

Speen hot Marshmallow Topping (see page 74) into a long glass and swirl around so marshmallow covers the inside. Shake ice cream and Big M together until frothy. Pour into prepared glass and serve.

CALYPSO COOLER
Makes 1 drink

¾ cup milk, chilled
3 tablespoons Calypso Cream

Shake or whisk together all ingredients. Serve chilled in a tall glass.

STRAWBERRY SIP
Makes 2 drinks

300 ml Big Strawberry M, chilled
⅓ cup sliced strawberries
3 tablespoons CocoRibe liqueur
1 scoop vanilla ice cream
¼ cup crushed ice

Blend all ingredients together until smooth. Serve in chilled glasses and sip through straws.

BANANA BENDER
Makes 2 drinks

300 ml Big Banana M, chilled
½ ripe banana
3 tablespoons Coffee Supreme
1 scoop vanilla ice cream
¼ cup crushed ice

Blend all ingredients together until smooth. Pour into tall glasses and serve.

CAFE ORANGE
Makes 1 drink

300 ml Big Iced Coffee M
1 tablespoon orange liqueur
lemon rind

Pour liqueur into a long heatproof glass. Heat Big M until nearly boiling. Remove from fire and beat until frothy. Pour on to liqueur and top with a little finely grated lemon rind.

FIRELIGHTER
Makes 1 drink

1 cup hot milk
1 tablespoon CocoRibe
2 teaspoons Grenadine liqueur
nutmeg

Mix CocoRibe and Grenadine liqueur in a shaker, add hot milk and shake. Pour into a heatproof glass. Sprinkle nutmeg over the top and serve piping hot.

An unusual mixture of coconut and pomegranate, makes a delightfully different drink for a cold winter's night. Try it after the theatre — it's a great nightcap.

IRISH COFFEE
Makes 1 drink

1 cup black coffee
2 tablespoons Irish Mist liqueur
1 tablespoon thickened cream,
   lightly whipped

Pour steaming coffee into a tall, heatproof glass or cup. Stir in Irish Mist. Pour whipped cream over the top.
Serve immediately.

To keep the cream on top of the coffee, pour slowly over the back of a spoon.

TIPSY CHOCOLATE
Makes 1 long drink

¾ cup milk, chilled
2 tablespoons Creme de Cacao
1 scoop ice cream, vanilla or
   chocolate

Blend all ingredients together.
Serve in a long glass with a straw.

BOOZY BANANA
Makes 1 long drink

300 ml Big Banana M, chilled
2 tablespoons Island Cream liqueur
1 scoop ice cream, vanilla, banana,
   or chocolate

Blend all ingredients together until frothy. Pour into a long glass and serve with a straw.

SKINNY CHOCOLATE THICK SHAKE
Makes 2 drinks

500 ml Skinny, chilled
4-6 tablespoons chocolate topping
  or sauce

Beat ¾ cup of Skinny with chocolate until very thick and frothy. A rotary beater, blender or food processor will thicken the ingredients quickly. With the machine still running on high, slowly pour in the remaining Skinny.

Serve over ice cubes in two long glasses while still frothy.

PINEAPPLE MINT COOLER
Makes 2 drinks

500 ml milk
1 cup canned crushed pineapple
2 fine slices orange
2 fine slices lemon
2 sprigs mint
castor sugar

Blend pineapple, undrained, and milk until smooth. Taste and add sugar if desired. Pour into two long glasses. Decorate with slices of orange and lemon. Dip mint into iced water, shake off excess, and dip into castor sugar. Float on top of milk.

Serve with straws.

STRAWBERRY MILK ROMANOFF
Makes 2 long drinks

600 ml Big Strawberry M, chilled
2 scoops Smoothy vanilla or
  strawberry ice cream
4 tablespoons whipped cream,
  flavoured with Orange Curacao
2 whole strawberries

Beat Big M and ice cream together and pour into 2 long glasses. Spoon cream over the top and garnish with strawberries.

Serve with straws.

Photographed L. to R.
Strawberry Milk Romanoff
Skinny Chocolate Thick Shake
Pineapple Mint Cooler
(see all recipes this page).

HOT CHOCOLATE M
Makes 1 long drink

300 ml Big Chocolate M
5 marshmallows
1 teaspoon Kahlua

Snip marshmallows into quarters and drop into the bottom of a long, heatproof glass. Pour over Kahlua. Heat Big M till nearly boiling. Pour over marshmallows.
Delicious to sip through the melted marshmallows.

DUTCH HOT CHOCOLATE
Makes 1 cup

¾ cup Smoothy
2 teaspoons cocoa
sugar to taste

Mix cocoa and sugar with 2 tablespoons Smoothy in a cup. Heat Smoothy until nearly boiling. Pour into cup. Stir and serve.

MOCHA NIGHTCAP
Makes 2 short drinks

300 ml Big Iced Coffee M
2 teaspoons cocoa
2 teaspoons brandy

Heat Big M. Mix cocoa and brandy together in the bottom of two cups. When just boiling, pour into cups, stir and serve.

ANGEL'S DREAM
Makes 1 drink

1 cup Smoothy
½ teaspoon instant coffee powder
30 g cooking chocolate
1 tablespoon whisky

Break chocolate into squares. Heat Smoothy, chocolate and coffee together in a small saucepan until nearly boiling. Pour whisky into a long heatproof flask. Top up with hot ingredients and serve.

MISTLETOE
Makes 1 drink

300 ml Big Egg Flip M, chilled
2 tablespoons Irish Mist liqueur

Shake or whisk Big M and liqueur together and pour into a long glass.

SMOOTHY ICED COFFEE
Makes 1 long drink

¾ cup Smoothy, chilled
2 teaspoons instant coffee powder
2 teaspoons hot water
sugar to taste
1 scoop vanilla ice cream

Dissolve coffee in hot water in a glass and add the sugar. Stir in Smoothy and vanilla ice cream.
Serve chilled.

HOT BUTTERED RUM
Makes 1 long drink

1 cup milk
1½ tablespoons rum
2 teaspoons brown sugar
1 teaspoon butter
cinnamon stick
nutmeg

Heat milk. Mix sugar and rum together in the bottom of a tall, heatproof glass. Pour hot milk into glass. Stir with cinnamon stick. Drop butter on the top of the hot milk. As it melts, sprinkle nutmeg over the top.
Note: Milk pans are easier to clean if first rinsed out with cold water before heating milk.
If you don't have heatproof glasses, place a metal spoon into the glass and pour the hot milk over the spoon. This way you will avoid breaking the glass.

BLUSHING JAMAICAN SPIDER
Makes 1 drink

1 scoop vanilla ice cream
2 tablespoons Calypso Cream liqueur
1 tablespoon cherry brandy
200 ml lemonade, chilled

Place ice cream (see page 15) in a long glass. Pour over liqueurs. Pour in half the lemonade and stir. Then top up slowly with remaining lemonade.
Second half of lemonade must be poured slowly, otherwise it will froth up and overflow.

ORANGE FLUFF
Makes 4 drinks

¼ cup milk
1½ cups orange juice
1 egg white
2 tablespoons sugar
5 ice cubes

Blend all ingredients together in a food processor or blender until ice is crushed. Serve immediately.

SERENISSIMA
Makes 1 drink

1 scoop Liqueur Ice Cream
2 tablespoons Creme de Cacao
200 ml lemonade, chilled

Place Marsala (Liqueur) Ice Cream (see page 38) in a long glass. Pour over liqueurs. Pour in half the lemonade and stir. Then top up slowly with remaining lemonade.

HANNIBAL'S REVENGE
Makes 1 drink

½ cup milk
3 tablespoons Irish Mist liqueur
ice

Shake milk with Irish Mist liqueur. Pour over ice into a short glass and serve.

SKINNY SOURBALL
Makes 1 cocktail

½ cup Skinny
2 ice cubes
1 tablespoon apricot brandy
2 teaspoons lemon juice
2 teaspoons orange juice

Shake all ingredients together until frothy. Strain into cocktail glass and serve immediately.

This is a delightfully refreshing cocktail which is light and sufficiently tart to whet the appetite without ruining it as so many other cocktails do.

If left to stand separation can occur, but it does not affect the flavour of the drink.

If making this up in large quantities for a party, use a blender and strain out any remaining ice before serving. If left to stand, simply blend again to reconstitute before serving.

PEACH AFFAIR
Makes 1 drink

1 cup Skinny, chilled
2 canned peach halves, drained
2 teaspoons glucose powder
1 teaspoon wheatgerm

Blend all ingredients together until frothy. Serve immediately in a long glass.

Note: Left to stand, this drink separates — it doesn't affect the enjoyment of the drink and in fact, it is quite delicious sipping the milk through the peach froth.

SURFERS SWINGER
Makes 1 drink

1 scoop pineapple ice cream
1½ tablespoons gin
2 teaspoons orange Curacao
200 ml lemonade, chilled

Place pineapple ice cream (see page 58) in a long glass. Pour over liqueurs. Pour in half the lemonade and stir. Then top up slowly with remaining lemonade.

TAHITIAN BREEZE
Makes 1 cocktail

1 tablespoon Smoothy
¼ cup pineapple juice, chilled
¼ cup CocoRibe liqueur
cherry

Shake Smoothy with pineapple juice and CocoRibe liqueur. Pour into chilled cocktail glass. Garnish with a cherry.

DAIRY FIZZ
Makes 2 cocktails

¾ cup Smoothy, chilled
80 ml (4 tablespoons) gin
2 tablespoons orange concentrate
2 egg whites
dash orange flavouring
crushed ice
nutmeg

Blend all ingredients, except nutmeg, together in a food processor, blender or shaker till creamy and frothy. Strain into two short glasses. Sprinkle nutmeg on the top and serve.

MAURITIUS COCKTAIL
Makes 1 cocktail

⅓ cup Smoothy
1 tablespoon CocoRibe liqueur
Grenadine syrup, a dash
ice
nutmeg

Over ice, mix CocoRibe liqueur and a dash of Grenadine syrup with Smoothy. Shake well. Strain off ice and serve in a cocktail glass. Garnish with nutmeg. Serve immediately.

SMOOTHY GRASSHOPPER COCKTAIL
Makes 1 cocktail

2 tablespoons Smoothy
⅓ cup Grasshopper liqueur
ice
1 teaspoon thickened cream, whipped
Maraschino cherry

Mix Grasshopper and Smoothy with lots of ice. Stir or shake until cocktail is well chilled. Strain into a cocktail glass. Garnish with a teaspoon of cream and top with a cherry.

BRANDY ALEXANDER
Makes 1 cocktail

⅓ cup Smoothy, chilled
1 tablespoon brandy
1 tablespoon thickened cream
nutmeg

Mix brandy with Smoothy. Shake well, pour into cocktail glass. Garnish with thickened cream and grate nutmeg over the top.

Photographed L. to R.
Mauritius Cocktail
Smoothy Grasshopper Cocktail
Brandy Alexander
(see all recipes this page).

Index

GLOSSARY

For a description of milk products see page 6.

The various liqueurs, spirits and grenadine syrup are available at liquor outlets.

AERATING — Lightening with air, usually by the addition of whipped egg whites or cream in ice creams, or by beating and freezing.

ALMOND MEAL — Very finely ground almonds, available at supermarkets and specialized food stores.

ALMONDS, FLAKED — Fine slices cut across the kernel, which is usually blanched first. Available from health food stores and specialized food stores.

ALMONDS, SLIVERED — Strips cut from the length of the kernel. Available supermarkets, health food stores and specialized food stores.

AMARETTI BISCUITS — Are Italian almond-flavoured biscuits, available in some supermarkets and continental outlets.

ANGELICA — Refers to crystallised stems of the angelica plant, which has an unusual flavour and is excellent for garnishes. Most commercial angelicas are dyed celery parading under a false name.

BLANCH — To whiten. To blanch almonds, cover with boiling water and slip off the skins when soft.

BLEND — To mix together.

BLOOD TEMPERATURE — Is when a mixture feels neither hot nor cold to the touch.

BUTTER BRAZIL NUTS — Brazil kernels with an outer coating of butterscotch toffee, available at sweet stores, supermarkets and delicatessens.

CALVADOS — Brandy distilled from apples.

CANISTER — The inner container which holds the ice cream mixture in the ice cream churn.

CARAMEL — Refers to sugar and usually water, when boiled to a dark brown colour and a toffee consistency. A sugar thermometer should register 160°C (320°F).

CARAMELISE — Means to cook to a reduced consistency when all moisture evaporates and ingredients turn brown.

CARAWAY SEEDS — Seeds used as a spice from the caraway herb; it is a cousin of anise, dill and fennel and is used widely in German and Austrian cooking.

CHARLOTTE MOULD — A plain deep mould with sloping sides, which, when inverted, the top makes a wide firm base.

CHESTNUT PUREE — Often referred to as Marron, the French name, is mostly imported in cans and is sometimes sweetened and flavoured with vanilla. Available from some supermarkets and continental outlets.

CITRUS PRESS — A citrus juicer which operates on leverage releasing the juices and the essences in the fruit skins.

CHANTILLY CREAM — Cream whipped to a mousse-like consistency, sweetened and flavoured with vanilla or other flavourings.

CHRISTMAS MINCE MEAT — Known as Mince Meat, the English version has no meat in it. Made with a mixture of minced fresh and dried fruits, suet, sugar and alcohol and spices. Especially popular at Christmas time in England, it is customarily served in little pies. American Mince Meat, does in fact include meat.

COEUR A LA CREME MOULDS — Heart shaped moulds used for a classic French dessert which is a kind of sweet cream cheese shaped like a heart. Made in ceramic they are useful for many other recipes. They are available in two sizes at gourmet cook ware shops and department stores.

CRANK — Means to churn.

CROCCANTINO — Is the Italian name given to a recipe which includes almond sweetmeats or almond biscuits.

CULTURE — Refers to the "starter" yoghurt used to begin a new batch of yoghurt. Sometimes called sub-culture.

CURDLE — To coagulate or separate. This separation of fats and solids occurs when acids are mixed with dairy products and in over-heating as with an egg-based custard.

DASHER — The paddle which mixes the ingredients in an ice cream churn.

DICE — To cut into cubes.

DIFFUSER — A utensil designed to spread heat evenly between the heat source and the cooking utensil. Available at good cookware outlets.

DREDGE — To sprinkle.

ENHANCE — To intensify the flavour.

ENRICH — To make rich or to enhance.

FLAME and FLAMBÉ — Means to flame or to cook over heat.

FOOD MILL — Is a sieve, which is highly efficient, and makes purees very smooth.

FOOD PROCESSOR — A machine which blends, purees, chops, slices and grates, minces and mixes, at an extremely fast speed. It is the revolutionary kitchen machine of the decade.

FOOL — Is the name given to an old-fashioned dessert which consists of pureed fruits, sweetened and stirred into whipped cream or custard, in the proportion of two to one. It should be served in a tall glass.

FREEZE/BEAT — Refers to a method of setting iced mixtures. Freeze mixture until partially set, usually about one third from the top edge, removing from the freezer, beating, then returning to the freezer until set firm.

GARNISH — To decorate.

GIANDUIA — Refers to an Italian flavouring of chocolate powder and hazelnuts.

GLACE MARRONS — Chestnuts, glaced and packed in cans or jars. Usually imported and available from continental outlets and some supermarkets.

HOMOGENISED MILK — Milk which is made more digestible by distributing the fat globules evenly throughout the milk.

HULL — To remove the green calyx and stem from the top of the fruit as with strawberries.

IGNITE — To set alight.

INCUBATE — The term used in yoghurt-making when an even heat is used to foster the development of bacteria.

INFUSION — Liquid poured over ingredients and sometimes heated, in order to extract flavours.

INVERT — To turn upside-down.

IMMERSE — To cover with liquid.

JULIENNE — To cut into fine matchsticks.

LASAGNE DISH — A rectangular, shallow dish which is oven-proof.

MACERATE — Means to soften by soaking.

MARSALA — A light wine similar to sherry, from Marsala in Sicily. A locally-made product is available.

TO MATURE — Means to fully develop flavours.

MEMBRANES — Refers to the fibrous skins separating the segments in fruits, like citrus fruits.

PARE — Means to peel using a small paring knife, (vegetable knife) or a vegetable peeler.

PISTACHIOS — Are brilliant green kernels with a unique flavour, which are usually sold salted. This can be washed off during blanching and skinning. Lose their colour when stale.

PITH — Is the soft white tissue between the skin and flesh of fruits, it is usually bitter.

PLUMPED — Refers to ingredients which have been swelled in a liquid, usually warmed.

POPSICLES — Icy poles.

PRALINE POWDER — Almonds and caramelised sugar, set together and then pounded to a powder. Sometimes made with other kernels.

PULVERISE — Means to reduce to a powder.

PUREE — Reduce to a pulp.

RECEDING — Shrinking.

RECONSTITUTE — To restore to original condition.

RIBBONING — Refers to the stage at which a mixture forms a ribbon pattern when the beaters are lifted above the ingredients.

RIPEN — Means to freeze to a firmer consistency in order to improve texture. An efficient freezer will take up to two hours to ripen an iced mixture, but a freezer compartment in a refrigerator could take six hours, or overnight.

RISING AGENTS — Used when plain flour and other non-rising flours are required when the recipe needs to expand and rise. Cream of tartar, baking powder and bicarbonate of soda are the most commonly used.

ROOM TEMPERATURE — Refers to the average heat inside a house or kitchen. 21°C (70°F) is an excellent temperature to work with.

ROTARY BEATER — Manually-operated with two beaters geared to work together in a rotary motion. It is inexpensive, easy to use and available at hardware stores, supermarkets, cookware shops and department stores. Commonly called an egg beater.

SAVARIN MOULD — Is a ring-shaped mould which is usually used for a yeast dough mixture.

SHRED — To cut or scrape into strips.

SOFT PEAKS — The stage often referred to in egg white and cream work, when the mixture should stand freely in soft peaks without collapsing.

SOLIDIFY — To set solid.

SORBETIERE — The French name for an ice cream churn.

SPATULA — A flat utensil used for lifting foods, also useful for scraping and folding.

SPIDER — Is the name given to a soda fountain drink, consisting of ice cream, lemonade and flavouring.

SPRING FORM — A cake pan with removable sides and base.

STARTER — Refers to the yoghurt reserved specially for starting a new batch. See culture.

STERILISE — To destroy micro organisms.

TAINT — Refers to imparting a taste or scent to food.

TARRAGON — A herb with a sweetish yet slightly bitter taste, which should be used sparingly. It tastes a little like anise. Franch tarragon is better for culinary uses than the Russian.

TURBOT SHAKER — Is a clear beaker, with curved vanes in the inverted cones on the base and lid, which, when shaken, propels the liquids around inside. Excellent for making dairy drinks and available at most cookware outlets.

WATER BATH — Correctly termed a Bain Marie it is a container filled with water, in which another container is placed. It is used to slow down the cooking or melting process where there is a danger of over heating and spoiling.

WETTED MOULD — Is one which has been rinsed out with cold water without drying to prevent food from sticking.

WOODEN SPATULA — Used in place of a wooden spoon. It is straight with no concave spoon to catch sticky ingredients and is better for getting into corners than a spoon.

ZABAGLIONE — An Italian dessert flavoured with Marsala, called Sabayon in France.

WEIGHTS AND MEASURES

Recipes in this book use the standard metric equipment approved by the Australian Standards Association, with the exception of temperatures which give the imperial equivalents in brackets.

METRIC CUP AND SPOON MEASURES ARE USED AND ALL INGREDIENTS ARE LEVELLED OFF.

A set of metric cup and spoon measures will greatly assist. They are available at hardware and kitchenware shops.

CUP SIZES (DRY MEASURE)
A standard metric cup set consists of 1 cup, ½, ⅓, and ¼ cups.
Scoop ingredients into cup and level off without packing down.

SPOON SIZES
The basic spoon sizes are:
the tablespoon (20 ml)
the teaspoon (5 ml)
½ and ¼ teaspoons complete the set.
All are used as level measures.

JUG SIZES (LIQUID MEASURE)
These are graduated.
The litre is marked at every 100 ml and at every metric cup (250 ml). The metric cup is graduated every 50 ml and at the ¼, ⅓, ½, ⅔, ¾, and 1 cup marks.

FOR QUICK REFERENCE
1 cup = 250 ml
½ cup = 125 ml
⅓ cup = 83 ml
¼ cup = 62.5 ml

1 tablespoon = 20 ml
1 teaspoon = 5 ml
½ teaspoon = 2.5 ml
¼ teaspoon = 1.25 ml

OTHER METRIC UNITS
1 kilogram (kg) = 1000 grams (g)
(1 kg = approx. 2¼ lbs)
1 Litre (L) = 1000 millilitres (ml)
(⁴/₇ of a litre = 1 pint)
1 centimetre (cm) = 100 millimetres (mm)
(2½ centimetres = approx. 1'inch)

CATERING SUGGESTIONS
Recipes in this book may be doubled or halved with equally successful results to the final product.
When catering for large groups it is not necessary to double the ingredients in order to serve double the number. For instance if you treble a recipe which originally serves 8, it will serve up to 30 and not just 24.
For ice cream and yoghurt, a generous ½ cup (150 ml) is an average serve for one person. This is equal to about 5 ozs.